An SPSS Companion for the Third Edition of The Fundamentals of Political Science Research

An SPSS Companion for the Third Edition of The Fundamentals of Political Science Research offers students a chance to delve into the world of SPSS using real political science data sets and statistical analysis techniques directly from Paul M. Kellstedt and Guy D. Whitten's best-selling textbook.

Built in parallel with the main text, this workbook teaches students to apply the techniques they learn in each chapter by reproducing the analyses and results from each lesson using SPSS. Students will also learn to create all of the tables and figures found in the textbook, leading to an even greater mastery of the core material.

This accessible, informative, and engaging companion walks through the use of SPSS step-by-step, using command lines and screenshots to demonstrate proper use of the software. With the help of these guides, students will become comfortable creating, editing, and using data sets in SPSS to produce original statistical analyses for evaluating causal claims. End-of-chapter exercises encourage this innovation by asking students to formulate and evaluate their own hypotheses.

Paul M. Kellstedt is Professor of Political Science at Texas A & M University. He is the author of *The Mass Media and the Dynamics of American Racial Attitudes* (Cambridge, 2003), winner of Harvard University's John F. Kennedy School of Government's 2004 Goldsmith Book Prize. In addition, he has published numerous articles in a variety of leading journals. He is the Editor-in-chief of *Political Science Research and Methods*, the flagship journal of the European Political Science Association.

Guy D. Whitten is Cullen-McFadden Professor of Political Science, as well as Director of the European Union Center, at Texas A & M University. He has published a variety of articles in leading peer-reviewed journals. He is on the editorial boards of *Electoral Studies* and *Political Science Research and Methods*.

An SPSS Companion for the Third Edition of The Fundamentals of Political Science Research

Paul M. Kellstedt
Texas A & M University

Guy D. Whitten
Texas A & M University

CAMBRIDGE
UNIVERSITY PRESS

CAMBRIDGE
UNIVERSITY PRESS

University Printing House, Cambridge CB2 8BS, United Kingdom

One Liberty Plaza, 20th Floor, New York, NY 10006, USA

477 Williamstown Road, Port Melbourne, VIC 3207, Australia

314–321, 3rd Floor, Plot 3, Splendor Forum, Jasola District Centre,
New Delhi – 110025, India

79 Anson Road, #06–04/06, Singapore 079906

Cambridge University Press is part of the University of Cambridge.

It furthers the University's mission by disseminating knowledge in the pursuit of
education, learning, and research at the highest international levels of excellence.

www.cambridge.org
Information on this title: www.cambridge.org/9781108447935
DOI: 10.1017/9781108594615

First published 2020

A catalogue record for this publication is available from the British Library.

ISBN 978-1-108-44793-5 Paperback

Additional resources for this publication at www.cambridge.org/FPSRspss

BRIEF CONTENTS

CONTENTS

PREFACE

We received a wealth of useful feedback from instructors and students about the first two editions of *The Fundamentals of Political Science Research*. In response to feedback on the first edition, we substantially increased the number of end-of-chapter exercises in the second edition. While the response to this increase was positive, we sensed a demand for even more exercises and, in particular, more hands-on material for how to put the techniques that we discuss in the book into action. This workbook is our attempt to meet these demands. It is one of three workbooks, each written to help students to work with the materials covered in the third edition of *The Fundamentals of Political Science Research* using a particular piece of statistical software.

This workbook focuses on using the program SPSS. Our expectation is that the modal user of this book will be using a relatively recent version of SPSS on a computer that is running some version of the Windows operating system. We also have made an effort to accommodate users who are using some version of macOS or OS X. A webpage available at www.cambridge.org/fpsr will help Mac users with any difficulties.

The chapter structure of this workbook mirrors the chapter structure of the third edition of *The Fundamentals of Political Science Research*. We have written with the expectation that students will read the chapters of this companion after they have read the chapters of the book.

We continue to update both the general and instructor-only sections of the webpage for our book (www.cambridge.org/fpsr). As before, the general section contains data sets available in formats compatible with SPSS, Stata, and R. The instructor-only section contains several additional resources, including PowerPoint and TEX/Beamer slides for each chapter, a test-bank, and answer keys for the exercises.

Paul M. Kellstedt
Guy D. Whitten

FIGURES

1 THE SCIENTIFIC STUDY OF POLITICS

1.1 OVERVIEW

In this chapter we introduce you to some of the important building blocks of a scientific approach to studying politics. As you can already tell from reading the first chapter of the third edition of *The Fundamentals of Political Science Research* – which we will refer to as "*FPSR*" from here on – data are an important part of what we do both to explore the political world and to test hypotheses based on causal theories. An important part of working with data is learning how to use a statistical software package. In the sections that follow, we introduce you to the SPSS program and some basics that you will need to get up and running. In doing this, we also introduce some general principles of good computing practices for effectively working with data.

1.2 "A WORKBOOK? WHY IS THERE A WORKBOOK?"

You might be asking yourself this question, and it's perfectly fair to do so. Allow us to try to explain how this workbook fits in with the main *FPSR* text.

As you will see in the weeks and months to follow in your class, the main textbook will teach you about the use of statistics in political science, mostly by using equations and examples. So yes, in some ways, it will feel rather math-y. (And we think that's cool, though we realize that it's not everyone's cup of tea.) One of the ways that people learn about the practice of statistics is to use computer software to calculate statistics directly. To that end, many instructors want students to learn to use a particular computer software package so they can begin to conduct statistical analyses themselves.[1] We have discovered through years of teaching that this transition between equations in a book and software output on a computer screen is a very difficult one. The goal of this software companion book is to make this connection stronger, even seamless.

If we are successful, this book will do two things. First, it will teach the nuts and bolts about how to use SPSS. Though many (perhaps most) students today are quite computer-literate, we believe that having a reference guide for students to learn the techniques, or for them to teach themselves out of class time, will be helpful. Second, and more importantly, this software guide will provide explicit hand-holding to you as

---

[1] This particular software companion book teaches students to use SPSS, but we have also produced parallel books for instructors who wish to have their students learn Stata or R.

you learn to connect the key principles from the main text to the practical issues of producing and interpreting statistical results.

Each chapter of this software guide works in parallel with that of the main *FPSR* text. So when you learn the equations of two-variable regression analysis in Chapter 9 of the main text, you will learn the details about using SPSS to estimate two-variable regression models in Chapter 9 of this companion book. And so on. In the end, we hope that the very important (but perhaps rather abstract) equations in the text become more meaningful to you as you learn to estimate the statistics yourself, and then learn to interpret them meaningfully and clearly. Those three things – formulae, software, and interpretation – together provide a very solid foundation and basic understanding of social science.

Let's start.

1.3   GETTING STARTED WITH SPSS

To get started with SPSS, we recommend that you set yourself up in front of a computer that has the program installed with a copy of *FPSR* close by. You should also have the set of computer files that accompany this text (which you can download from the text's website, www.cambridge.org/fpsr) in a directory on the computer on which you are working. You will get the most out of this workbook by working in SPSS as you read this workbook.

The instructions in this book can help you learn SPSS whether you use a Windows-based PC or a Mac. Once the program is launched, SPSS works identically, no matter which platform you use. Mac users should be aware, though, that our screenshots will come from a Windows-based PC. Some of those screenshots that involve finding and opening files on your computer, therefore, will look somewhat unfamiliar to Mac users, but we assume that Mac users are at least somewhat used to this. Overall, the differences between running SPSS on Windows compared to a Mac are minimal.

Finally, we wrote this book while using version 25 of SPSS. Particularly for the statistical fundamentals you will learn in this book, the differences between versions – at least as old as SPSS 20 – are not severe. In fact, if you use any version of SPSS between 20 and 25, you might not notice the difference between what appears on your screen and what appears in the screenshots contained in this book.

1.3.1   Launching SPSS

When you are sitting in front of a computer on which SPSS has been properly installed, you can launch the program by double-clicking on the SPSS desktop icon (if one exists on your computer) or by finding the SPSS program on your Start menu, likely under "IBM SPSS Statistics." At this point, you should see one large window like that in Figure 1.1.

The large box in the middle of the screen enables you to open recent files that have been used on that computer. Since we assume that you're working on a lab or cluster computer, the simplest way to proceed is to simply close that window, either with the "Close" button in the lower-right corner or the "X" in the upper-right corner.

Figure 1.1   SPSS initial launch with recent files window

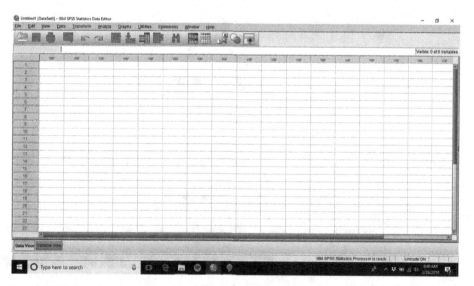

Figure 1.2   SPSS initial launch after closing recent files window

When you do that, you should see something very similar to what appears in Figure 1.2. It looks more or less like an empty spreadsheet, right? Some of the menu items (like "File" and "Edit") will look quite familiar, but others ("Transform," "Analyze," for example) will presumably be new to you. In addition, beneath the menu items, the row of icons will mostly appear unfamiliar – except, perhaps, the far-left icon that looks like an opening manila folder. If you are seeing all of this, you are ready to go.

The part of the screen that looks like an empty spreadsheet is meaningful, especially the "empty" part. As you might guess, that's where the data that we will be analyzing will appear. As you also might guess, we haven't loaded any data into SPSS yet, hence the "empty." We'll get there soon enough.

Figure 1.3 Opening a file with pull-down menu for "File," "Open," and "Data" selected

Figure 1.4 Pop-up menu for opening a file in SPSS

1.3.2   Getting SPSS to Do Things by Using Pull-Down Menus

We will accomplish the vast majority of the tasks in SPSS by using the pull-down menus you see across the top of Figure 1.2. In our first foray into the program, we are simply going to open a data set. This means that we need to start either by clicking on the textual heading "File," then "Open," and then "Data." In Figure 1.3, we show what this will look like. Alternatively, you can just click on the icon that looks like a folder being opened, right below "File." Either way, you'll see a pop-up box open up that looks like what we see in Figure 1.4.

Figure 1.5 Navigating directory paths in SPSS to open a file

Once you have done this, you will need to direct SPSS to the location on your computer where you have placed the *FPSR* SPSS companion files. (As we noted above, these can be downloaded from www.cambridge.org/fpsr.) Throughout this workbook, on the computer on which this workbook was created, these files are located in the directory "C:\MyFPSRSPSSFiles." To navigate to that folder, we use the pull-down menu as in Figure 1.5, and then change the drive and directory as necessary until we find the correct location where the data set is stored.

The initial data set that we wish to open is named "EcoVote.sav," so once we see that file, as you can in Figure 1.4, we click on "EcoVote.sav" and then click the "Open" button. The ".sav" portion of the file name denotes that the file is in the format of an SPSS data set.[2]

You may have noticed that, when you opened the data set, SPSS launched an additional window. This is an important part of how SPSS works. When you execute a command in SPSS, it appears in what we will call the "output window." You can toggle back and forth between the main window and the output window by hovering over the SPSS icon in your task tray in Windows. Figure 1.6 shows the main window of SPSS with the output window layered on top of it. Every command you run in SPSS will generate some type of output, and all of that output will be shown in that output window. You will be able to edit the output – we'll show you how to do that eventually. This happens frequently, actually, even with experienced data analysts, because we often

---

[2] Like most software programs, SPSS can import data sets that are created with other types of software. To do that, you would click "File," "Import data," and then choose the format that you're trying to import and follow along as pop-up boxes open. If you want to continue to use imported files in SPSS, you might wish, once a file is imported, to "Save As" an SPSS .sav file. ("Save As" is also under the "File" menu.)

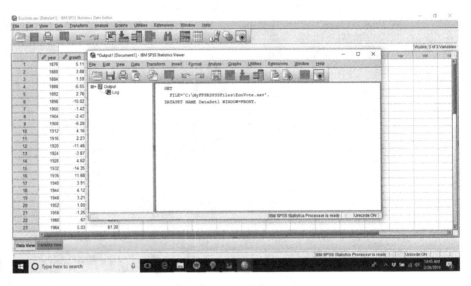

Figure 1.6 Opening a data set and launching the output window

Figure 1.7 Main window view of the "EcoVote.sav" data set

run some type of data analysis and then realize we wished we had done something else. Saving or printing the results of the output window is also easy, and we'll show you how to do that, too.

For the moment, let's simply minimize the output window by just clicking on the "_" (minimize) portion of the output window near the top-right. That will leave us with the main SPSS window where we will eventually do our analysis. That view is displayed in Figure 1.7.

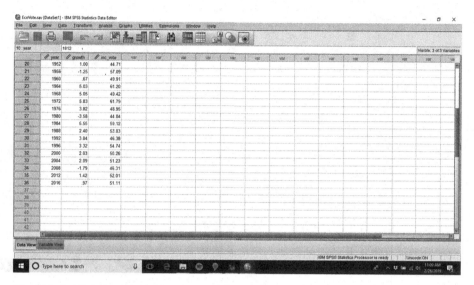

Figure 1.8 Scrolling down to the bottom of the "EcoVote.sav" data set

1.3.3   Initially Examining Data in SPSS

Now that we have shown you how to get data into SPSS, we want you to take a look at the data that you have loaded into the program.[3] These data are from a famous study of economic voting conducted by Ray Fair (Fair 1978). They contain values of economic growth and incumbent party vote from US presidential elections between 1876 and 2016.

In Figure 1.7, you will see data in three columns, labeled from left to right as "year," "growth," and "inc_vote." Those labels correspond to the names of the three variables in our data set. Down the rows, you will see the cases of the three variables. For example, in row 10 of the data window, which is the tenth case in the data set, we see the following values for the three variables. "Year" takes on the value of "1912," "growth" has the value of "4.16," and "inc_vote" has the value 54.71. From the discussion in Chapter 1 of *FPSR*, can you guess what these three variables represent, and what the corresponding values mean?

You can use the bars at the right and at the bottom of the data set to scroll through it. As you already know, this data set has only three variables, so there is no need to scroll to the right to see any other variables. However, you can use the bar at the right of the screen to scroll down, as we do in Figure 1.8. There, you'll notice that the last of our cases is for the year 2016, with a value for "growth" of 0.97 and a value for "inc_vote" of 51.11. You can see that the bottom row of our data set is row 36, which means that our data set of US presidential elections consists of 36 cases.

---

[3] We discuss how to manually enter your own data into an SPSS file in a webpage, available at www .cambridge.org/fpsr.

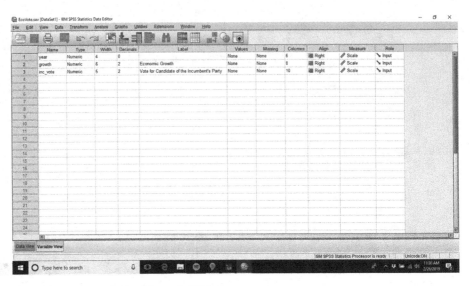

Figure 1.9 The "Variable View" feature in SPSS

In the lower-left portion of Figure 1.8, you will notice that there are two tabs – on the left, in a peach-like color, is "Data View" (the view that is currently active, as you might guess, because you're viewing the data), and on the right, in light blue, is "Variable View." Click on the "Variable View" tab. You will notice a few things, including that the colors have reversed themselves, with the "Data View" now in light blue, and the "Variable View" in peach. More importantly, we are no longer looking at the columns of data, but instead at the description of the variables in the data set. It should look like Figure 1.9.

Several things are worth mentioning. First, the variable names that were formerly across the top in columns under the "Data View" are now down the left in rows in "Variable View." And there are details about what each of those variables means. In particular, notice the "Label," "Values," and "Missing" columns. The "Label," as you might guess, is the label of the variable. The variable "year" does not even have a label (it is fairly self-explanatory). The labels for "growth" and "inc_vote," respectively, are "Economic Growth" and "Vote for Candidate of the Incumbent's Party." So we no longer have to guess what the variables mean. The labels tell us. Also, under "Values" and "Missing," you will note that all of the cells say "None." The "Values" option will be useful later on, and we will refer to it frequently in this book. There are no labels for the values here, because for all three variables, the values speak for themselves. If, for any of the cases, we could not obtain data for any reason for the values of a variable, we would need a category for that to let SPSS know that the value is missing. Typically, researchers use a value like "−9999" to denote a missing case. If any of our variables had missing cases, and the "Missing" cell for that variable read "−9999," then SPSS

Figure 1.10 How to save your output in SPSS

would know to conduct whatever analysis using that variable without making reference to that particular case. Again, these features will come into play in subsequent chapters with other data sets.

1.3.4   Saving Output and Exiting the Program

To save the results of our output window, from Figure 1.6, we can just click on the icon that looks like an old-style floppy disk, or click on "File," followed by "Save." One thing to note is that SPSS will not default to saving your output in the same place where the data are stored, so use the pull-down menu as above to find the correct drive and directory where you want your output saved. Your screen should look similar to Figure 1.10.

Another caution: SPSS defaults to saving its output as an "SPSS Viewer File," which means you can only see it on a computer that has an SPSS license on it. So if you were to save your output from a lab onto a memory stick or a folder in the Cloud, you would only be able to view the output if you were on another computer with an SPSS license. As a result, we recommend using the pull-down menu next to the "Save as type" option, and saving files as .html files (what SPSS will call an "SPSS Web Report"). That detail is displayed in Figure 1.11.

You can exit SPSS by clicking the "X" in the top-right of the program, and it will prompt you to see if you're sure you want to exit, and if any file changes need to be saved.

You are now ready to proceed to the end-of-chapter exercises.

Figure 1.11 How to save your output in SPSS as an .html file

1.4   EXERCISES

1. Go through all of the steps described above. Once you have the "Data View" open (so that your computer looks like Figure 1.7), do the following:

    (a) Look at the values in the column labeled "growth." This is Fair's measure of percentage change in real GDP per capita. Do the following:

        i.   Identify the year with the highest value for this variable.
        ii.   Identify the year with the lowest value for this variable.
        iii. What does it mean if this variable goes up by 1?

    (b) Look at the values in the column labeled "inc_vote." This is Fair's measure of the percentage of major party votes cast for the party of the president at the time of the election. Now do the following:

        i.   Identify the year with the highest value for this variable.
        ii.   Identify the year with the lowest value for this variable.
        iii. What does it mean if this variable goes up by 1?

2 THE ART OF THEORY BUILDING

2.1 OVERVIEW

One of our emphases in the book has been on producing new causal theories, and then evaluating whether or not those theories are supported by evidence. In this chapter, we describe how to explore sources of variation – both across space, and across time – to get you started thinking about new explanations for interesting phenomena. We also help you explore how new theories can be built upon the existing work in the literature.

2.2 EXAMINING VARIATION ACROSS TIME AND ACROSS SPACE

As we discuss in Section 2.3 of *FPSR*, one way to develop ideas about causal theories is to identify interesting variation. In that section, we discuss examining two types of variation, cross-sectional and time-series variation. In this section, we show you how to create figures like the ones presented in Section 2.3 of *FPSR*. Although there are many different types of graphs that can be used to examine variation in variables, we recommend a bar graph for cross-sectional variation and a connected plot for time-series variation.

2.2.1 Producing a Bar Graph for Examining Cross-Section Variation

A useful way to get a sense of the variation for a cross-sectional variable is to produce a bar graph in which you display the values of that variable across spatial units. In the example that we display in Figure 2.1 of *FPSR*, we have a bar graph of military spending as a percentage of gross domestic product in 2005 for 22 randomly selected nations. Building on what we learned in Chapter 1, we will now show you how to produce a figure like this in SPSS. The first step to doing this is opening the data.

As was the case in Chapter 1, all of the data files that we will use are located in the directory "C:\MyFPSRSPSSFiles" on the computer that created this workbook. We encourage you to follow this practice for the sake of convenience. To navigate to that folder, we use the pull-down menus – "File" then "Open" then "Data" – as described in Chapter 1, and then change the drive and directory as necessary until we find the correct location where the data set is stored. The data file is called "milspend_pct_05.sav." Once you've found it, open it.

Figure 2.1 First view of the military spending data set

Your screen should look like Figure 2.1. So let's build a graph like the one in Figure 2.1 of *FPSR*.[1] We build a graph in SPSS using the "Graphs" command at the top of the toolbar. So click on "Graphs," and in the pull-down menu, click on "Chart Builder...." At this point, a dialog box might open cautioning you to be careful about measurement levels of your variables. If so, click "OK" to proceed.

The "Chart Builder" dialog box will appear, as in Figure 2.2. As you can see from Figure 2.1 in the main text, we want to build a bar chart here. In SPSS's Chart Builder, we choose the type of chart – Bar, Line, Histogram, etc. – from the lower-left pane of the dialog box. The "Bar" option should be the default choice. (If something else happens to be selected on your screen, though, click on "Bar" on the lower-left under the "Gallery" tab.) The next tab to the right is the "Basic Elements" tab, where we define what we want our bar graph to look like. Click on "Basic Elements." When you do that, you'll see the sub-tabs, one in which we will "Choose Axes," and the other in which we will "Choose Elements."

As you will see, there are several options for each category, and they are displayed here in Figure 2.3. Under "Choose Axes," we want a simple two-dimensional $X-Y$ chart, so double-click on the top-right of those five choices (as seen in Figure 2.3). Under "Choosing Elements," we want bars, so double-click the option that looks like vertical bars. Please note that it's essential to double-click both of these options, not merely click on them once.

Double-clicking both of those decisions of "Basic Elements" will produce a screen that looks like that in Figure 2.4. You'll see a rudimentary bar chart in the top-left pane

---

[1] You might notice that the graph we produce here will not look exactly like the one in the main textbook, and that's okay in this case. That figure was generated using a different software program, so we will be doing our best to approximate that figure. This issue will crop up repeatedly throughout this workbook, and we encourage you to not worry about it. In fact, what you'll almost universally notice is that the output is remarkably similar – just not identical.

Figure 2.2 SPSS's Chart Builder

Figure 2.3 The "Basic Elements" tab of SPSS's Chart Builder

of the dialog box. But we haven't yet told SPSS what variables we want in the chart. Let's do that now.

As you can see from Figure 2.1 of the main text, the *x* axis variable is the nation, and the *y* axis variable is the amount of military spending as a percentage of GDP. We define those variables in the chart by grabbing them with our mouse from the list of variables in the top-left of the dialog box and dragging them to the appropriate (*x* or *y*) axis and dropping them there. So go ahead and do that. Grab the variable labeled "Military Expenditures as a Percentage of GDP [milspend_pct]" and drag and drop it onto the *y* (vertical) axis. Next, grab the variable labeled "nation" and drag and drop it onto the *x* (horizontal) axis.

Figure 2.4 Selecting the "Basic Elements" in SPSS's Chart Builder

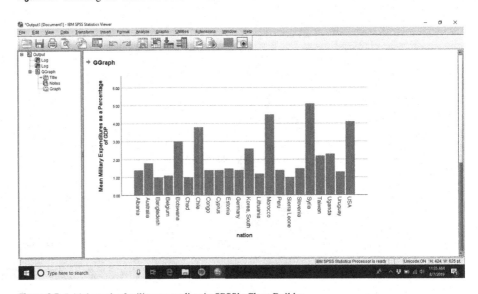

Figure 2.5 Initial graph of military spending in SPSS's Chart Builder

Now let's see what this looks like, just as a first cut, and note how it compares to Figure 2.1 in the main text. Click on the "OK" button at the bottom of the dialog box and let's find out. You will notice that the output window appeared, and a command sequence appears, and the graph (though you might have to scroll down to see it). Sometimes it helps to maximize the output window to get a fuller view, as we have done in Figure 2.5.

In the output window, if you left-click your mouse one time inside the graph, it selects the entire graph. Then, if you right-click your mouse once, you'll be able to copy it to your computer's clipboard, and paste it elsewhere (like a word processor) if you need to.

Alternatively, if you right-click, you will also see the option to "Export..." the graph. You can export the file to a Word document, an Excel spreadsheet, an Adobe .pdf file, or (if you select the "None (Graphics only)" option) you can export the graph as a high-resolution graphics image such as a .png, .tif, .bmp, or .jpg file (among other types).

Now let's compare Figure 2.5 with Figure 2.1 in *FPSR*. What is the difference between these two figures? The most obvious answer is that in Figure 2.1 in *FPSR* the values of military spending have been sorted from smallest to largest, whereas in the bar graph we have made, they are sorted alphabetically. When displaying data in graphs, it is important that you do so in a fashion that allows you and your readers to most easily make the assessments that you and they want to make. In this case, since we are trying to think about what makes a country spend more or less of its GDP on its military, we want to be able to see which countries spend more or less. Try comparing the value of military spending between Belgium and Lithuania in the graph that we just made, Figure 2.5. Not an easy thing to do! It's a lot easier using Figure 2.1 from *FPSR* because the cases have been *sorted*.

SPSS allows us to sort the bars to our liking. To do so, from the output window where we see our bar chart, double-click the chart, which will launch "Chart Editor" mode. That appears in Figure 2.6. Because we want to change the *x* axis, we click on the blue "X" in the toolbar to "Select the *x* axis." From there, select the "Categories" tab; then, under "Sort by," use the pull-down menu to select "Statistic"; then click "Apply" and then "Close." You will notice that, when we click the "X" in the top-right corner to close our Chart Editor, our edited chart now appears in our SPSS output. From here, you can also save or export the graph in the same way as mentioned above.

At this point, we're reasonably close to exactly reproducing Figure 2.1 from *FPSR*. You will notice a few small differences, though, and you could experiment with the Chart Editor to rectify those differences should you care to do so.

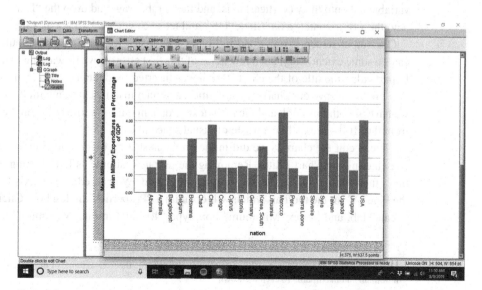

Figure 2.6 Launching SPSS's Chart Editor

2.2.2   Producing a Connected Plot for Examining Time-Series Variation

A useful way to get a sense of the variation for a time-series variable is to produce a connected plot in which you display the values of that variable *connected* across time. In the example that we display in Figure 2.2 of *FPSR*, we have a connected plot of the values for presidential approval each month from February 1995 to December 2005. Building on what we learned in Chapter 1, we will now show you how to produce a figure like this in SPSS. As with the previous example, the first step to doing this is to load the data into SPSS.

Because we already have data from the previous example in active memory, we first have to tell SPSS that we want to use a different data set. We do that by using the "File" menu, then "New" and "Data," and the previous example's data are removed.

Again, the data are located in the directory "C:\MyFPSRSPSSFiles" on the computer that created this workbook. To navigate to that folder, we use the pull-down menus – "File" then "Open" then "Data" – and then change the drive and directory as necessary until we find the correct location where the data set is stored. The data file is called "presap9505.sav." Once you've found it, open it.

As before, we'll build a graph in SPSS using the "Graphs" command at the top of the toolbar. So click on "Graphs," and in the pull-down menu, click on "Chart Builder...." Again, if a dialog box opens cautioning you to be careful about measurement levels of your variables, click "OK" to proceed. The "Chart Builder" dialog box will appear.

As you can see from Figure 2.2 in the main text, we want to build a line chart here. So, in Chart Builder, we choose the type of chart – in this case "Line" – from the lower-left pane of the dialog box. In the "Line" box, there are two types. Double-click the one on the left – "Simple Line" – and SPSS will begin to build the chart.

Your screen should look like that in Figure 2.7. Next, in the top pane of the Chart Builder, let's define the axes. Grab, drag, and drop the "presap" variable from the variable list onto the *y* (vertical) axis, and then grab, drag, and drop the "Date" variable onto the *x* (horizontal) axis. Click "OK" and let's see what we've got as a first cut.

Our output screen is presented in Figure 2.8. Tastes for how a graph should appear can (to some extent) vary, but a few items of this first effort leave us wanting to do better. In particular, the title of the chart (which was inserted by default) is a bit cumbersome. (We prefer to leave our charts without titles, and then insert a caption with the figure, as we have in both this book and the main text.) Also, in our view, the range on the *y* axis – from 0 to 100 – seems like a waste of visual space to us.[2]

We can edit the chart as we did in the previous section by double-clicking the chart and entering the Chart Editor. Removing the title is as simple as left-clicking on it one time, then hitting the Delete key on your keyboard. We can edit the *y* axis by hitting the blue "Y" in the toolbar, which will open up a "Properties" dialog box. Click on the "Scale" tab, and in the "Minimum" box, type "40," and in the "Maximum" box, type

---

[2] Others might like the 0–100 range, because it represents the true theoretical range of the variable's minimum and maximum. To each their own.

Figure 2.7 Beginning to build a line graph using SPSS's Chart Builder

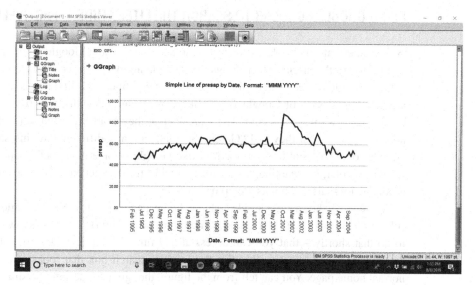

Figure 2.8 A first cut at a line graph of presidential approval

"90." Click "Apply," and then "Close," and you have (in our eyes) a much better-looking chart. It should look like our screen in Figure 2.9.

At this point, we're reasonably close to exactly reproducing Figure 2.2 from *FPSR*. As before, you can also save or export the graph in the same way as mentioned above.

In Chapter 1, we will introduce you to a series of commands associated with time-series data and some other ways in which to produce graphs of time-series data.

Figure 2.9 A better (to us) line graph of presidential approval

2.3   USING GOOGLE SCHOLAR TO SEARCH THE LITERATURE EFFECTIVELY

We assume that you're skilled at web searches, likely using Google's search engine. In addition to the myriad other things that Google allows us to search for on the internet, it has a dedicated search engine for scholarly publications like books and journal articles. The aspects of Google you're likely most familiar with come from Google's home page – www.google.com. The searches that they enable through scholarly work, however, using what they call "Google Scholar," are at a different site: https://scholar .google.com. That site looks a good bit like Google's home page, but when you're at Google Scholar, it's searching a different corner of the internet entirely – the part where academic journals and books are uploaded.

Figure 2.10 shows the Google Scholar home page. If you have a Google account (like a Gmail address), you can save items in "My Library" – we'll show you how to do that shortly – that you can access at any time. The articles are normally saved as an Adobe .pdf file. You'll notice the familiar search box that looks like Google's normal home page. You can tell from the figure, though, that, despite the similarities in appearances, this website is https://scholar.google.com.

So let's see how Google Scholar works. In the first chapter of *FPSR*, we introduced you to what we called the theory of economic voting. The seminal article in the study of economic voting was conducted by an economist named Ray Fair. So let's see what happens when we type "Ray Fair economic voting" in the Google Scholar search bar.

Figure 2.11 shows the results of that Google Scholar search. As luck would have it, the first search result happens to be that path-breaking article. Let's examine that result. If you look to the far right of the selection, you see the text "[PDF] jstor.org," which shows you what format the file is available in – in this case, an Adobe .pdf – and where – in this case, at the archive www.jstor.org. Your college or university's library

Figure 2.10 The Google Scholar home page

Figure 2.11 Google Scholar results for "Ray Fair economic voting" search

almost surely has a subscription to JStor that your student fees pay for, and so if you're on a campus internet connection (as opposed to a Wi-Fi network at your home, or on a cellular network), clicking on "[PDF] jstor.org" will take you to the article. (If you're on your home Wi-Fi network, then JStor doesn't know that you're a university student, and the publisher might ask you to pay a rather steep fee for access to the article. So beware about where you can do these searches for free.)

There's a lot of other information that the Google Scholar search reveals, though. First, if you want to save the Ray Fair article to your "My Library," then click on the ★ at the lower left of the item, and you'll be able to access that .pdf anywhere.

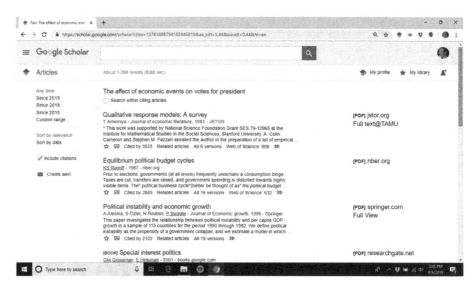

Figure 2.12 Google Scholar search results of articles citing Ray Fair (1978) article

Importantly, you can also see how influential every article has been to date. In Figure 2.11, you can see text near the bottom of the citation that says "Cited by 1098" – which means that the Fair article has been cited 1098 times to date.[3] That number indicates that the paper has been massively influential.[4]

Of course, that doesn't necessarily mean that 1098 other articles all cite the Fair article approvingly. Some might; others might not. But being agreed with, or being "proved right," isn't the highest value in science. It's far better to be an influential part of an ongoing debate while being proved wrong in some respects, than it is to be indisputably correct but ignored by other scholars.

Perhaps you say to yourself, "Sure, Professor Fair wrote an influential article on economic voting a good long while before I was born. What kind of work is being done on the topic *now*?" This is one of the places where Google Scholar is fabulous. That "Cited by 1098" is clickable. You can literally see the list of all 1098 articles that cite the Fair article if you want. (Of course, it would take you a while to sift through them!)

Figure 2.12 shows the results when you click the "Cited by 1098." Now click the "Since 2018" option on the left side of the screen. (You can pick "since" any year you like, obviously.) Just beneath the search bar, you'll see the text in light gray saying "About 53 results," indicating that, since 2018, the Fair article has been cited by 53 other articles. So it continues to have influence today.

---

[3] If you conduct that same search today, the number would surely be higher; our search was conducted on August 6, 2019. Citations tend to accumulate over time.

[4] Of course, you should be careful to remember the original publication date when interpreting citation counts as a measure of impact. Fair's article was published in 1978, so it's not as if some scholars who work in this area have somehow not yet heard of his article. But for an article published more recently – say in 2016 – its impact cannot yet fully be known. That merely means that we don't yet know if the article is likely to have a large impact. Only time will tell.

This is a good way to start the process of exploring a particular topic in academic writing that interests you. This example began by having us tell you that the initial article that spawned all of this interest was written by Ray Fair. So we incorporated his name, obviously, into the search terms. Often, to be sure, this isn't the case.

Just like with using any internet search engine, there's something of a skill in figuring out how to efficiently search for the material you want without getting bogged down with lots of results that aren't interesting to you. Should you use quotation marks in your search, or in a portion of your search terms? Sometimes yes, sometimes no. (In the example above, we did not.) As a general rule, it might be best to try it both ways to see if you get different results.

We have not exhausted all there is to know about how to use Google Scholar here, of course. For example, many scholars have created "Google Scholar profiles," which enable you to see the list of scholarly articles and books that they have authored, usually sorted from those with the most citations to the ones with the least. This can help you find similar articles, too, because many scholars work on a topic over the course of many years, and therefore their earlier articles are related to their more recent ones. In Figure 2.12, for example, you can see the scholars whose names are underlined; those are clickable links to those scholars' respective Google Scholar profiles. In addition, the "Help" section of Google Scholar is surprisingly helpful![5]

2.4   WRAPPING UP

In the main text, we discussed how important it is that our theories be new and original – that is, that we aren't merely repeating the ideas and claims of previous scholars. One of the important preconditions for doing something genuinely new is to be familiar with the works that have already been produced on that same topic. Having the vast archive of journal articles and even many books available online – and freely accessible, thanks to your university's libraries – through storage sites like www.jstor.org has been the first step in making this task a lot easier than it was in decades past. The second step has been the invention of very sophisticated search engines like Google Scholar to help us find the previous studies that we otherwise might have missed.

2.5   EXERCISES

1.   Conduct a search for the following terms using both Google's home page (www
     .google.com) and Google Scholar (https://scholar.google.com). Only include the
     quotation marks in your search if we include them. Report the similarities and
     differences you observe in the first page of the search results:
     (a)   "presidential approval"
     (b)   "nuclear proliferation"
     (c)   nuclear proliferation

---

[5] In light gray text, you can see the "Help" link that you can click in the bottom-right of Figure 2.10.

2.   Launch SPSS and open the "milspend_pct_05.sav" data set.

    (a)   Once you have done this, follow the steps above to reproduce – as nearly as possible – the graph presented in Figure 2.1 from *FPSR*. Open a word processing document and then copy the figure from SPSS and paste it into your word processing document.

    (b)   Write a short summary of what you see in this figure.

3.   Launch SPSS and open the "presap9505.sav" data set.

    (a)   Once you have done this, follow the steps above to reproduce – as nearly as possible – the graph presented in Figure 2.2 from *FPSR*. Open a word processing document and then copy the figure from SPSS and paste it into your word processing document.

    (b)   Write a short summary of what you see in this figure.

3 EVALUATING CAUSAL RELATIONSHIPS

3.1 OVERVIEW

Unlike the previous two chapters, in Chapters 3 through 5, there will not be any computer-based lessons in SPSS or elsewhere. Not to worry, though. There will be more than enough time for intensive computer work later in the book. We promise!

In this abbreviated chapter, then, we offer some expanded exercises that will apply the lessons learned in the main text, and build on the skills from the first two chapters.

3.2 EXERCISES

1. Causal claims are common in media stories about news and politics. Sometimes they are explicitly stated, but often they are implicit. For each of the following news stories, identify the key causal claim in the story, and whether, based on the information given, you are convinced that all four causal hurdles have been crossed. (But remember that most media stories aren't the original generators of causal claims; they merely report on the news as they see fit to do so.)

   (a) www.cnn.com/2018/01/16/politics/freedom-house-democracy-trump-report/index.html

   (b) https//thehill.com/opinion/energy-environment/368355-wheres-the-proof-climate-change-causes-the-polar-vortex

   (c) www.foxnews.com/us/2018/01/16/california-mudslides-where-and-why-happen.html

   (d) www.aljazeera.com/news/2018/01/trump-muslim-ban-shifted-public-opinion-study-finds-180113092728118.html

   (e) www.npr.org/player/embed/575959966/576606076 (Podcast)

2. Candidates for public office make causal claims all the time. For each of the following snippets from a key speech made by a candidate, identify the key causal claim made in the speech, and whether, based on the information given, you are convinced that all four causal hurdles have been crossed. (But remember that candidates for office are not scientists responsible for testing causal claims; they are trying to persuade voters to support them over their opponent.)

   (a) "America is one of the highest-taxed nations in the world. Reducing taxes will cause new companies and new jobs to come roaring back into our country. Then we are going to deal with the issue of regulation, one of the greatest job-killers of them all. Excessive regulation is costing our country as much as $2 trillion a year, and we will end it. We are going to lift the restrictions on the production of American energy. This will produce more than $20 trillion in job-creating economic activity over the next four decades." (Excerpt from Donald Trump's speech accepting the Republican nomination for President, July 21, 2016.)

(b)   "Now, I don't think President Obama and Vice President Biden get the credit they deserve for saving us from the worst economic crisis of our lifetimes. Our economy is so much stronger than when they took office. Nearly 15 million new private-sector jobs. Twenty million more Americans with health insurance. And an auto industry that just had its best year ever. That's real progress." (Excerpt from Hillary Clinton's speech accepting the Democratic nomination for President, July 28, 2016.)

(c)   "The truth is, on issue after issue that would make a difference in your lives – on health care and education and the economy – Sen. McCain has been anything but independent. He said that our economy has made 'great progress' under this president. He said that the fundamentals of the economy are strong. And when one of his chief advisers – the man who wrote his economic plan – was talking about the anxiety Americans are feeling, he said that we were just suffering from a 'mental recession,' and that we've become, and I quote, 'a nation of whiners.'" (Excerpt from Barack Obama's speech accepting the Democratic nomination for President, August 28, 2008.)

(d)   "His [Barack Obama's] policies have not helped create jobs, they have depressed them. And this I can tell you about where President Obama would take America: His plan to raise taxes on small business won't add jobs, it will eliminate them; ... And his trillion-dollar deficits will slow our economy, restrain employment, and cause wages to stall." (Excerpt from Mitt Romney's speech accepting the Republican nomination for President, August 30, 2012.)

3.   Political science, as we have argued, revolves around the making and evaluation of causal claims. Find each of the following research articles – Google Scholar makes it easy to do so – and then identify the key causal claim made in the article. Then produce a causal hurdles scorecard, and decide to what degree you are convinced that all four causal hurdles have been crossed. Some of the statistical material presented in the articles will, this early in the semester, be beyond your comprehension. That will change as the semester rolls along! (And remember that political scientists are trained to be experts in testing causal claims. So set the bar high.)

(a)   Heberlig, E., Hetherington, M. and Larson, B. 2006. "The price of leadership: Campaign money and the polarization of congressional parties." *Journal of Politics* 68(4): 992–1005.

(b)   Stasavage, D. 2005. "Democracy and education spending in Africa." *American Journal of Political Science* 49(2): 343–358.

(c)   De Mesquita, B.B., Morrow, J.D., Siverson, R.M. and Smith, A. 1999. "An institutional explanation of the democratic peace." *American Political Science Review* 93(4): 791–807.

(d)   Lipsmeyer, C.S. and Pierce, H.N. 2011. "The eyes that bind: Junior ministers as oversight mechanisms in coalition governments." *Journal of Politics* 73(4): 1152–1164.

4 RESEARCH DESIGN

4.1 OVERVIEW

As was the case in Chapter 3, there will not be any computer-based lessons in SPSS or elsewhere. Again, we offer some expanded exercises that will apply the lessons learned in the main text.

4.2 EXERCISES

1. There are a lot of substantive problems in political science that we might *wish* to study experimentally, but which might seem to be impossible to study with experimental methods. (Recall from the main text (Section 4.2.4) that one of the drawbacks to conducting experiments is that not all X variables are subject to experimental control and random assignment.) Imagine the following causal questions, and write a paragraph about what would be required to conduct an experiment in that particular research situation, being careful to refer to both halves of the two-part definition of an experiment in your answer. (Warning: Some of them will seem impossible, or nearly impossible, or might require time travel.)

    (a) Does the development of state-sponsored universities cause economic development to rise?

    (b) Has the establishment of independent central banks to control monetary policy caused a reduction in the severity of recessions?

    (c) Does an individual's religiosity cause a person's level of opposition to same-sex marriage?

    (d) Does a country's openness to trade cause blue-collar workers' wages to fall?

    (e) Does having a more professionalized legislature cause states to respond more quickly to voters' preferences?

    (f) Does having a more racially diverse set of school administrators and teachers cause a reduction in student suspensions and expulsions?

2. For each of the above research situations, if you were *unable* to perform an experiment, name at least one Z variable that could potentially confound the X–Y relationship, and would need to be controlled for in some other manner, in an observational study.

3. Assuming that you were unable to conduct an experiment for the aforementioned research situations, describe an observational study that you might conduct instead. In each case, is the study you envision a cross-sectional or time-series observational study? Why?

4. Consider the following research question: Does exposure to stories in the news media shape an individual's policy opinions?

    (a) Write a short paragraph trying to explain the causal mechanism that might be at work here.

    (b) If we wanted to study this relationship using an experiment, what would the barriers to conducting the experiment be?

    (c) What, if any, are the ethical considerations involved in studying that relationship experimentally?

    (d) What are the benefits of exploring that relationship experimentally? In other words, what specific Z variables would be controlled for in an experiment that could potentially be confounding in an observational study?

    (e) Read the following article and write a one-paragraph summary of it:

    • King, G., Schneer, B. and White, A. 2017. "How the news media activate public expression and influence national agendas." *Science* 358(6364): 776–780.

5. Consider the relationship between the level of democracy in a country and the country's respect for human rights.

    (a) Describe both a cross-sectional and a time-series observational design that would help test the theory that increase in the level of democracy causes a country to increase its respect for human rights.

    (b) What concerns would you have about crossing the four causal hurdles in each case?

6. Using the model described in Section 4.4 of the main text, write a one-paragraph summary of the following research articles:

    (a) Stasavage, D. 2005. "Democracy and education spending in Africa." *American Journal of Political Science* 49(2): 343–358.

    (b) O'Brien, D.Z. 2015. "Rising to the top: Gender, political performance, and party leadership in parliamentary democracies." *American Journal of Political Science* 59(4): 1022–1039.

    (c) Fortunato, D., Stevenson, R.T. and Vonnahme, G. 2016. "Context and political knowledge: Explaining cross-national variation in partisan left–right knowledge." *Journal of Politics* 78(4): 1211–1228.

(d)   Titiunik, R. 2016. "Drawing your senator from a jar: Term length and legislative behavior." *Political Science Research and Methods* 4(2): 293–316.

(e)   Bansak, K., Hainmueller, J. and Hangartner, D. 2016. "How economic, humanitarian, and religious concerns shape European attitudes toward asylum seekers." *Science* 354(6309): aag2147.

5 MEASURING CONCEPTS OF INTEREST

5.1 OVERVIEW

As was the case in Chapters 3 and 4, there will not be any computer-based lessons in SPSS or elsewhere. Again, we offer some expanded exercises that will apply the lessons learned in the main text.

5.2 EXERCISES

1. Consider, for a moment, the concept of "customer satisfaction." For now, let's define it as "the degree to which a product or service meets or exceeds a customer's expectations." So, like other concepts, it is a variable: Some customers are very satisfied, some have mixed experiences, and some are very unhappy. Companies – and even some government agencies – are interested for obvious reasons in understanding that variation. Now answer the following questions:

    (a) How well do you think Yelp reviews serve as a measure of customer satisfaction? Explain your answer.

    (b) Read "The Happiness Button" in the February 5, 2018, issue of *The New Yorker*: www.newyorker.com/magazine/2018/02/05/customer-satisfaction-at-the-push-of-a-button. What are the strengths and weaknesses of the strategy pursued by HappyOrNot in terms of measuring the concept of customer satisfaction?

    (c) The article describes the push button measures of satisfaction at security checkpoints in London's Heathrow Airport. What are the strengths and weaknesses of such an approach? If, on a particular day, there was a higher share of "frown" responses, what would that tell (and what wouldn't that tell) to the officials at Heathrow?

2. The concept of "political knowledge" is a very important one in the study of public opinion and political behavior, as it lies at the heart of many influential theories of why citizens hold the opinions that they do, and why they vote the way that they do. Answer the following questions:

    (a) Conceptually, how would you define political knowledge? Try to be as specific as possible.

(b) Measuring political knowledge, as you might imagine, can be a bit tricky. For years, the American National Election Studies (ANES) measured the concept by asking a small list of factual questions about politics. The questions were of the form:

> "Now we have a set of questions concerning various public figures. We want to see how much information about them gets out to the public from television, newspapers and the like... [NAME] – What job or political office does he [or she] NOW hold?"

Survey respondents were not given a closed-ended list of response options from which to choose; instead, they were allowed to respond freely, and their responses were recorded verbatim. After the survey was completed, coders would look at the response transcript and judge whether the answers were correct or not. A respondent's score on the political knowledge scale, then, would be the sum total of the number of correct answers given. What are the various strengths and weaknesses of such an approach?

(c) Skim the following report from the ANES, which pertains to these types of survey questions: www.jstor.org/stable/pdf/24572671.pdf. What were the main problems identified with the survey items? What effects did it have in measuring political knowledge?

(d) In more recent surveys, the ANES has been asking different types of survey questions to measure political knowledge. These questions are closed-ended, and for most, respondents are given a fixed list of options from which to choose. Here are two examples from the 2012 survey:

> "On which of the following does the U.S. federal government currently spend the least?" [Response Options (in random order): Foreign aid; Medicare; National defense; Social security.]

> "For how many years is a United States Senator elected – that is, how many years are there in one full term of office for a U.S. Senator?" [No response options given; exact number recorded.]

What are the potential strengths and weaknesses of this revised strategy to measure political knowledge?

(e) Can you think of an alternative measurement strategy for this concept?

3. The concept of "consumer confidence" is important in the study of economics and political science, among other disciplines.

(a) Go to https://news.google.com and search for "consumer confidence" (and be sure to use the quotation marks). From the search results, pick a recent news article that discusses consumer confidence. (Print out the article and include it with your homework.) How well, if at all, does the article define consumer confidence, or how it is measured?

(b) From what you know, offer a conceptual definition of consumer confidence.

(c)   There are two major surveys in the US that measure consumer confidence on monthly intervals. One of them is the Survey of Consumers at the University of Michigan. They produce what they call an Index of Consumer Sentiment, which is composed of responses to five survey items. One of the five is as follows:

> "Looking ahead, which would you say is more likely – that in the country as a whole we'll have continuous good times during the next five years or so, or that we will have periods of widespread unemployment or depression, or what?"

What are the potential strengths and weaknesses of this survey question as one component of consumer confidence?

(d)   All five of the items in the Michigan Index of Consumer Sentiment can be found here: https://data.sca.isr.umich.edu/fetchdoc.php?docid=24770. How are the five items similar to one another, and how are they different from one another?

(e)   The complete monthly survey can be found here: https://data.sca.isr.umich .edu/fetchdoc.php?docid=24776. You will note that the survey does not contain *any* questions to measure a survey respondent's political beliefs or affiliations. Why do you think that is the case?

(f)   Can you think of any additional survey questions that might complement or replace the ones in the Michigan Index?

6 GETTING TO KNOW YOUR DATA

6.1 OVERVIEW

In this chapter we introduce you to the commands needed to produce descriptive statistics and graphs using SPSS. If you're feeling a little rusty on the basics of SPSS that we covered in Chapters 1 and 2, it would be good to review them before diving into this chapter.

In Chapter 6 of *FPSR* we discussed a variety of tools that can be used to get to know your data one variable at a time. In this chapter, we discuss how to produce output in SPSS to allow you to get to know your variables. An important first step to getting to know your data is to figure out what is the measurement metric for each variable. For categorical and ordinal variables, we suggest producing frequency tables. For continuous variables, there is a wide range of descriptive statistics and graphs.

6.2 DESCRIBING CATEGORICAL AND ORDINAL VARIABLES

As we discussed in Chapter 6 of *FPSR*, a frequency table is often the best way to numerically examine and present the distribution of values for a categorical or ordinal variable. We will learn how to do this using the data sets from the main text, which include the 2004 American National Election Study – a survey of public opinion taken during that year's presidential campaign.

As is our practice, the data are located in the directory "C:\MyFPSRSPSSFiles" on the computer that created this workbook. To navigate to that folder, we use the pull-down menus – "File" then "Open" then "Data" – and then change the drive and directory as necessary until we find the correct location where the data set is stored. The data file is called "ANES2004small.sav." Once you've found it, open it.[1]

Table 6.1 in the main text shows a frequency distribution for the variable representing an individual respondent's religious identification. In SPSS, we generate this frequency distribution using the pull-down menu through clicking "Analyze," then "Descriptive Statistics," then "Frequencies...." That will open a dialog box where we will choose which variables from the data set to analyze. A screenshot of that dialog box appears in Figure 6.1. The list of available variables to analyze – only two in this case – are on the left part of the dialog box. Hover your mouse over those variables to see their

---

[1] A reminder: All of the data sets we use can be found in the SPSS directory at www.cambridge.org/fpsr.

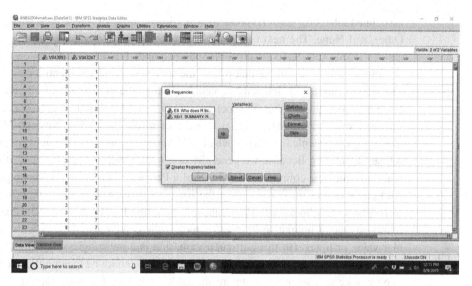

Figure 6.1   The dialog box of SPSS's Frequencies command

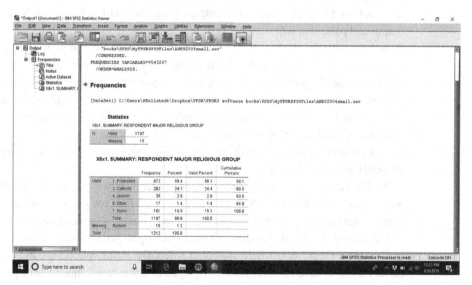

Figure 6.2   SPSS output of the Frequencies command

descriptions. The second of those, as you will discover, represents an individual's religious identification. Click on that, and then on the arrow button in the middle of the dialog box to select it. The variables in the right-hand box are the ones that will be analyzed.

We could click on the far right of the dialog box to select any statistics we'd like to see, to get a chart of the variables we analyze, and to edit the format and style of the results. More on this shortly. For now, however, just click "OK" and let's see the results.

Figure 6.2 shows the screenshot of the SPSS output. The figure contains several columns of information. The far-left column presents the numeric values and their associated labels for each respondent's religious group – Protestant, Catholic, Jewish, Other, and None. The next column, labeled "Frequency," contains the raw number of cases – in this case, individual people who responded to the survey – in each category; so, for example, you can see that 672 of the survey respondents identified as Protestant. The next column over, labeled "Percent," contains the percentage of all cases in each category; you can see that 55.4 percent of all cases identified as Protestant. Looking further down, you'll also notice that 1.2 percent are categorized as "Missing." Generally, that represents people in a survey who didn't know the answer to the question, or simply refused to answer. Because we generally don't want such cases to be part of our computations, the next column over is the "Valid Percent" – that is, the percentage of cases who chose one of the categories in the list of options. You'll notice that 56.1 percent of respondents who answered the question identified as Protestant. The final column represents the "Cumulative Percent," which is the percentage of cases with that particular value or lower. (In this particular case, that is a meaningless calculation, because religious identification is a categorical variable that cannot be meaningfully ordered.)

Now take a moment to compare the table in Figure 6.2 with Table 6.1 of *FPSR*. Although both tables convey the same information, Table 6.1 of *FPSR* does so in a more polished fashion. This is an example of why we don't want to copy from the SPSS output and paste that into our papers or presentations. It's worth noting that you can, as is the case with most output in SPSS, right-click in the table, and copy and paste it into a word processing program. But we hope that looking at that output shows why that's not a particularly good idea. The extra columns of output might be of interest to the analyst – you might care how many people refused to answer the question and became "missing" data – but they are almost certainly not of interest to your audience. Instead, it is important to craft tables so that they convey what is most necessary and don't include a lot of extra information. We'll have more to say about making tables in Chapter 8 (and forward) in this workbook.

Pie charts, such as Figure 6.1 in *FPSR*, are a graphical way to get to know categorical and ordinal variables. In SPSS, we can get a pie chart for our variable by using the same "Analyze," "Descriptive Statistics," "Frequencies..." procedure, and clicking on "Charts" to the right of that dialog box. It will open yet another dialog box like that presented in Figure 6.3, where we could select the radio button for "Pie charts." We could choose to have numeric values displayed as either raw frequencies or percentages. Once we've made our choice, click "Continue" and then "OK," and we'll see a pie chart in the output window. It looks nearly identical to the one in Figure 6.1 of the main text, though the legend is formatted and located differently. (As before, Figure 6.1 in the main text was generated using a different software program.) We can double-click on the graph to edit it if we choose to. You might notice in the output, for example, that SPSS has created a rather clunky looking title for the pie chart (without us asking for it) that reads: "X8x1. SUMMARY. RESPONDENT MAJOR RELIGIOUS GROUP." We might prefer a different caption, or none at all (in which case we could add a caption in our word processing software).

As you might guess, if we wanted a bar graph akin to the one in Figure 6.2 in the main text, we would just choose "Bar charts" instead of "Pie charts" in the dialog box for chart selection.

Figure 6.3 Obtaining a pie chart in SPSS as part of the Frequencies command

As we discuss in Chapter 6 of *FPSR*, statisticians strongly prefer bar graphs to pie charts because bar graphs make it easier to make assessments about the relative frequency of different values.

6.3   DESCRIBING CONTINUOUS VARIABLES

While the values for categorical variables in a sample of data can easily be presented in a frequency table, this is usually not the case for continuous variables. Consider Table 6.2 in *FPSR*, which contains 36 cases (each of which represents a US presidential election). Even for a relatively small data set such as this, the frequencies of each outcome in this output would be rather unwieldy. For this reason, we turn to summary statistics when we want to describe continuous variables. To use a metaphor, with summary statistics, we are looking at the broad contours of the forest rather than examining each individual tree.

To practice, let's use the data set on economic voting created by Ray Fair. As always, the data are located in the directory "C:\MyFPSRSPSSFiles" on the computer that created this workbook. To navigate to that folder, we use the pull-down menus – "File" then "Open" then "Data" – and then change the drive and directory as necessary until we find the correct location where the data set is stored. The data file is called "FairFPSR3.sav." Once you've found it, open it.[2]

Figure 6.3 in *FPSR* displays a full battery of descriptive statistics for the continuous variable *incumbent vote* (which we named "inc_vote" in the data set). We obtain SPSS's equivalent of that information by using the pull-down menu under "Analyze," "Descriptive Statistics," and then "Frequencies...," which opens up the familiar dialog box, and

---

[2] Again, all of the data sets we use can be found in the SPSS directory at www.cambridge.org/fpsr.

Figure 6.4 Details of the Descriptive Statistics command in SPSS, with several options selected

select variables as before. On the right of the dialog box, we choose the "Statistics" option to choose what statistics SPSS will generate for us.

As you see in our screenshot in Figure 6.4, there's a good number of options. And if you're a bit overwhelmed by the choices, perhaps you feel tempted to just check all of the boxes and figure out what information you need later on. (We've seen our students do that many times in our lab sessions!) You'll see from the detail in Figure 6.4 that we've selected many (but not all) of those options. Clicking "Continue" and then "OK" gets you the output. From the discussion in Chapter 6 of the main text, we can see that this command presents both rank statistics and moment statistics to describe the values taken on by continuous variables.

While statistical summaries of variables are helpful, it is also sometimes informative to also look at visual summaries of the values for a variable. To get a visual depiction of rank statistics, we recommend producing a box–whisker plot like that displayed in Figure 6.4 in *FPSR*. We make that chart using SPSS's Chart Builder, like we learned in Chapter 2 of this workbook. We begin by using the pull-down menu and selecting "Graphs" followed by "Chart Builder...." That opens up the Chart Builder dialog box, and from there, we begin in the lower-left portion, and click on "Boxplot" from the "Gallery" tab. Then double-click "Simple Boxplot," which activates the chart preview in the pane above. From the variable list in the top-left, grab and drag inc_vote onto the *y* (vertical) axis of the chart preview area. Then click "OK" to see our box–whisker plot.

Figure 6.5 displays SPSS's first attempt, and it's not bad. But we hope that you're growing accustomed to looking at these graphs with a critical eye, and a few details stand out to us as less than ideal. For example, the *y* axis reads "inc_vote," rather than "Incumbent Vote Percentage." And there's that pesky title that we didn't ask for – "Simple Boxplot of inc_vote" – across the top. As you can imagine, we can change these in the output window by double-clicking on the box–whisker plot and then

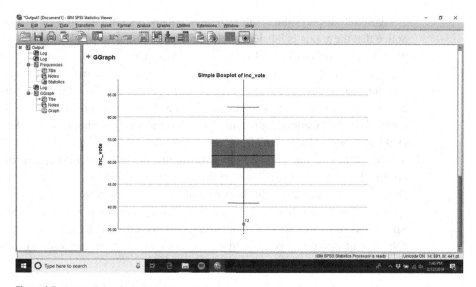

Figure 6.5 Output from the Boxplot command

Figure 6.6 A simple histogram from the Frequencies command

single-clicking on the title, then pressing the "Delete" key, and editing the *y* axis by double-clicking on that, and using our mouse and keyboard to edit the text into a more meaningful label.

To get a visual depiction of moment statistics, we recommend producing either a histogram – as in Figures 6.5 and 6.6 from *FPSR* – or a kernel density plot – Figure 6.7 from *FPSR*. We can obtain a simple histogram from the Frequencies command ("Analyze," "Descriptive Statistics," and then "Frequencies...") by clicking the "Charts" option and then selecting the radio button for "Histograms."

Figure 6.6 displays the resulting graph. Again, it's not bad, though we hope you'll notice that the *x* axis is labeled "inc_vote" in that less-than-helpful way. (You can edit this, as we've just described, by double-clicking on the chart in the output window.)

In this version of histograms, SPSS makes all of the decisions about the width of the bins for you. In case you'd like more control over the process, you can use the "Chart Builder" process that you've become familiar with, beginning with the "Histogram" option from the "Gallery" tab on the lower left part of the dialog box, and then double-clicking "Simple Histogram" from among the options. You would grab, drag, and drop the "inc_vote" variable onto the *x* axis. Customizing the bin widths happens by clicking on the "Element Properties" tab on the far right of the dialog box, then clicking the "Bar1" option under the "Edit Properties of" window. The button "Set Parameters" will open another dialog box, and then you can customize the bin width under the "Bin Sizes" portion of that window. For example, if you customize them and pick 10 as the "Number of intervals," you would end up with a histogram that looks very similar to the bottom panel of Figure 6.6 in *FPSR*.

6.4   PUTTING STATISTICAL OUTPUT INTO TABLES, DOCUMENTS, AND PRESENTATIONS

So you've generated some statistical output for the first time. Congratulations! But now what do you do? As you can tell from the descriptions above, we think it's important to be thoughtful about how to present your results to your audience. That's why we went to great lengths to show you commands to make the graphics appear in the most interpretable way possible. The same is true with data that you wish to include in a tabular format. We emphasize that just copying and pasting output from SPSS (or any other program) is unlikely to impress your audience – even if your audience is "just" your professor or teaching assistant.

For example, when we produce descriptive statistics in SPSS using the commands we described above, we tend to get a *lot* of output. Usually this output is much more than what we need to present in a paper that describes our variables one at a time. We therefore suggest making your own tables in whatever word processing program you are working with.

Graphs are a bit simpler, though. Once you have a graph that meets the standards we've outlined above, and you want to include it in a document, one of the easiest ways to do so is to right-click on the graph in SPSS and select "copy" and then right-click on the location where you want to place the graph in your word processing program and select "paste." Depending on the word processor, you might just want to re-size the graphic image by clicking on the corner of the image and dragging the image to be bigger or smaller, depending on what would look best in your paper or presentation.

We'll have more to say about this topic in Chapter 8, and forward, as we introduce new statistical techniques to you. The upshot, though, is always the same: Put some care into what you present to your audience. The amount of attention you devote to the details – great or small – will be obvious to your audience.

6.5   EXERCISES

1.   Launch SPSS and open the "ANES2004small.sav" data set. Once you have done this, follow the procedures described in this workbook chapter to produce the graphs presented in Figures 6.1 and 6.2 from *FPSR*. Open a word processing document and then copy these figures from SPSS and paste them into your word processing document.

2.   Using the same data set, run a Frequencies command for variable V043093, which is each respondent's prediction of who will win the 2004 US presidential election. In your word processing document, create a professional-looking frequency table like Table 6.1 from *FPSR* for variable V043093.

3.   Create a pie chart and a bar graph like Figures 6.1 and 6.2 from *FPSR* for variable V043093. Copy these figures from SPSS and paste them into your word processing document.

4.   Write a short summary of what you see in the table and figures that you created using variable V043093.

5.   Launch SPSS and open the "FairFPSR3.sav" data set. Once you have done this, follow the procedures described in this workbook chapter to create a box–whisker plot and a histogram for the variable "growth," which is the percentage change in real (meaning that this measure is adjusted for inflation) gross domestic product (GDP) per capita (meaning that it has been adjusted for population). Copy and paste each of these figures into your word processing document.

6.   Generate descriptive statistics for the variable "growth." Make a table in your word processing document which contains the moment statistics for this variable.

7.   Write a short summary of what you see in the table and figures that you created using variable "growth."

7 PROBABILITY AND STATISTICAL INFERENCE

7.1 OVERVIEW

In this chapter, we teach you how to use a computer simulation using a pre-programmed Excel spreadsheet. The goal of this chapter is to familiarize you with some of the basics of how probability works, and especially to see how sample sizes come into play.

7.2 DICE ROLLING IN EXCEL

There is a variety of free spreadsheets available online that simulate the rolling of dice.[1] The one we will use is available at the SPSS link at www.cambridge.org/fpsr.

Right-click on the filename "diceroller.xls" and save it to your computer.[2] Find the file and open it. What you'll see should look like Figure 7.1.

The spreadsheet is quite simple: It contains a basic program that simulates the rolling of two six-sided dice, with a graphic display of the resulting dice faces, as well as output data to keep track of the rolls. The sheet basically contains three sections. In the top-left of the sheet are the two dice. In the launch screen in Figure 7.1, those dice are a 5 and a 1. There are also buttons there to roll the dice – you can click the "Roll 'em (Ctrl+R)" button or press "Ctrl" and "R" on your keyboard. You can click the "Clear History" button to erase the history of rolls and start over.

The history of rolls of the two dice is displayed along the lower-left side of the sheet. In that section, there are columns of data to correspond to the roll number ("Roll #"), the roll of die 1 ("D1"), the roll of die 2 ("D2"), and the sum of die 1 and die 2 ("Tot"). In Figure 7.1, since we haven't rolled the dice yet, you will see that in the rows beneath the display of "Roll #, D1, D2, Tot," the cells are all empty. When we begin rolling the dice, those rows will begin to fill up.

The third section of the sheet, in the lower-right, shows the actual sum of the two dice (from the "Tot" column) – which will appear in red bars – as well as the distribution that we would *expect* to see given that the dice are fair – shown in gray bars.

Let's go ahead and roll the dice, either by hovering your mouse over the "Roll 'em" button and left-clicking it or hitting "Ctrl" and "R" on your keyboard. The results of

---

[1] Google "spreadsheet dice roller" to find several of them.

[2] Unfortunately, the functionality of the spreadsheet only works in Microsoft Excel, so if you're used to using Google Sheets, you'll need to be on a computer that has Microsoft Excel installed on it.

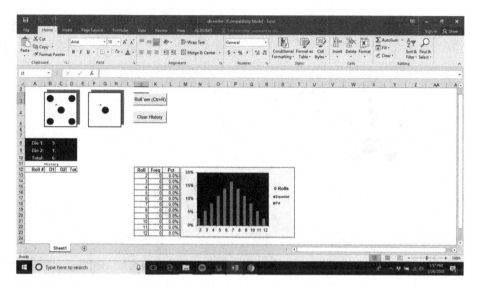

Figure 7.1 The dice roller in Excel

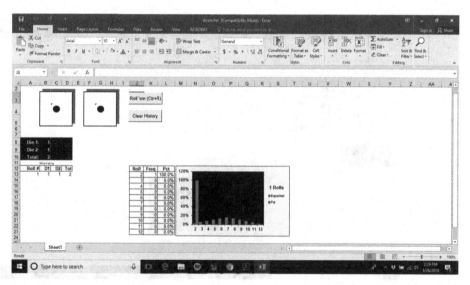

Figure 7.2 The results of our first roll

our first roll are in Figure 7.2. As you can see, we rolled a "snake eyes" – a 1 and a 1. (Obviously, when you're doing this on your own computer, you might roll something different!) All of the output looks as you'd expect. In the lower-left of the sheet, you see that, for roll 1, die 1 was a "1" and die 2 was also a "1," making the total (the sum) "2" (because 1 plus 1 equals 2). That's reflected in the graph on the lower-right portion of the sheet, with a large red bar at the spot for "2," indicating that all 100 percent of rolls so far totaled a "2."

Let's click "Roll 'em" a few more times, so that we get ten rolls in total.

Figure 7.3 shows the results of the first ten rolls that we performed when writing this chapter. (Again, the outcomes of your rolls are quite likely to be different from ours!)

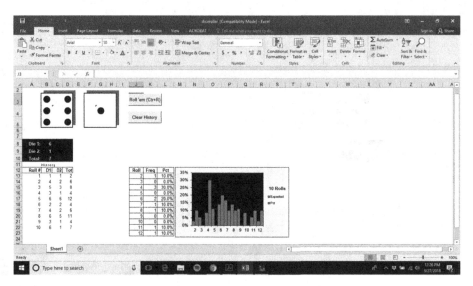

Figure 7.3 The results of our first ten rolls

Figure 7.4 The results of our first 100 rolls

You'll notice from the figure that we haven't rolled another "snake eyes." In fact, we've rolled three "4"s, two "6"s, and the other five results just one apiece.

We can roll the dice as many times as we'd like. (Just press "Ctrl" and "R" on your keyboard repeatedly. Yes, that means pressing it 100 times if you want 100 rolls, or 1000 times if you want 1000 rolls.) Go ahead and roll the dice around 100 times, and watch the red and gray bars shift as you do. (For our purposes right now, it doesn't matter if you roll them exactly 100 times.)

Figure 7.4 shows our results. As always, your rolls will be different from the ones we got. Let's examine the results in the figure. As you can see from the output screen and associated bar graph, we have rolled a total of 4 – through a 1 and a 3, or a pair of 2s, or a 3 and a 1 – 15 times out of 100. That's more than would be expected by chance. You can also see that we've managed to roll double 6s six times out of the 100 rolls – again, more than would be expected. Perhaps the biggest discrepancy between the observed outcomes in red and the expected ones in gray is in the rolls that total 8. For whatever reason, we rolled about half as many 8s as would have been expected by chance.

Let's be clear: None of the above is meant to imply a judgment – positive or negative – on what we've found. In theory, there are a squadpillion possible rolls of these two dice, and what we've just done is sample one, then ten, and then 100 of them. At the extreme, rolling the two dice just one time produced a rather odd – by definition! – "outcome." Every single roll (of that one roll!) was a 2! How weird is that? Of course, for a single roll, *any* outcome would have been "odd" in this sense. As we move from one roll to ten to 100, though, we start to see the beginning of convergence between what we observe and what we expect to observe. Will the observed outcomes ever *exactly* equal the expected ones? Probably not.

One other thing that Excel allows us to do is to calculate the averages of the rolls of the individual die, and of the dice collectively. Doing so is straightforward. For example, if we want to calculate the average of the rolls of die 1, we can go anywhere in the spreadsheet and type

```
=average(b13:b112)
```

and hit the "Enter" key on the keyboard. (You'll see that we performed this in cell b114, because it is below the bottom of the string of cells for which we are calculating the mean, with a single space in between the last cell of data – cell b112 – and where we want our mean to be displayed.) That process is displayed in Figure 7.5, before we hit the "Enter" key. When we hit the "Enter" key, of course, the result will appear.

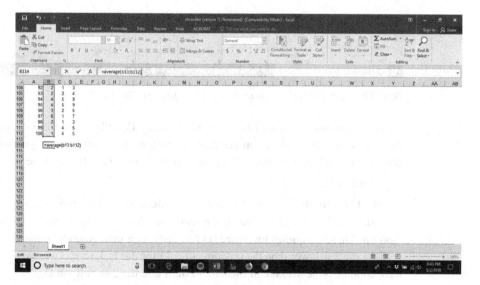

Figure 7.5 How to calculate the average of our first 100 rolls of die 1

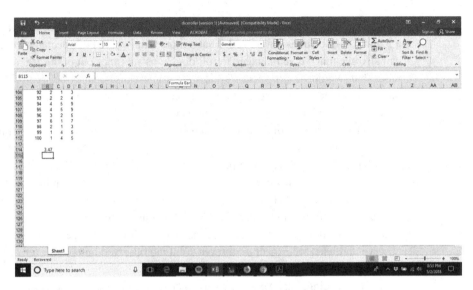

Figure 7.6 The result of calculating the average of our first 100 rolls of die 1

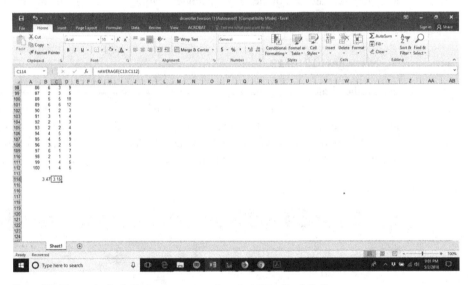

Figure 7.7 The result of calculating the average of our first 100 rolls of die 2

As you can see in Figure 7.6, the average of our 100 rolls of die 1 is 3.47. (We repeat the admonition that, when you perform this in your own spreadsheet, you will almost certainly get different results.) When we repeat the process – that is, type

```
=average(c13:c112)
```

in cell c114 – for die 2, we find a different result, as is evident in Figure 7.7.

That mean is 3.15. Does that figure seem "too low" to you? (And why did we type "too low" in scare quotes just there?) Obviously, in a mathematical sense, the result of 3.15 for die 2 is lower than the outcome of 3.47 for die 1: $3.15 < 3.47$, we all know. We have computed the average of the sum of die 1 and die 2 in column D.

Figure 7.8 The result of calculating the average of our first 100 rolls of the sum of die 1 and die 2

That result is displayed in Figure 7.8, and shows that the mean is 6.62. Because the mean of the rolls of die 1 is 3.47, and the mean of the rolls of die 2 is 3.15, the fact that the mean of the sum is 6.62 should not be surprising ($3.47 + 3.15 = 6.62$).

7.3 EXERCISES

1. In Figure 7.1 from the dice rolling module in Excel, before we actually roll any dice, what should we *expect* the mean of a set of rolls of a single die to be? Why? And what should we expect the mean of the sum of two rolls of dice to be? Why? How do these numbers compare to the outcomes we found in Figures 7.6, 7.7, and 7.8?

2. In Figure 7.2, you notice that we happened to roll two 1s. Given that, what is the probability of rolling two 1s on the next roll? Explain your answer.

3. You've surely noticed that the gray bars in the dice rolling module in Excel – representing the "expected" rolls – in all of the dice figures seem to be shaped almost like a normal distribution. Why is that? Be careful in answering this question, and try to be as explicit as possible in arriving at your answer.

4. If you haven't already, in the dice rolling module in Excel, roll your die 100 times. What are the means of die 1, die 2, and the sum of the two? How do these numbers compare to the outcomes we found in Figures 7.6, 7.7, and 7.8? What do you make of these similarities or differences?

5. Using the dice rolling module in Excel, roll the dice until the "observed" bars (in red) *roughly* approximate the gray "expected" bars. How many rolls did it take? Print out (or take a screen shot of) your output and turn it in with your answer.

8 BIVARIATE HYPOTHESIS TESTING

8.1 OVERVIEW

We are now ready to start testing hypotheses! As we discuss in Chapter 8 of *FPSR*, bivariate hypothesis tests, or hypothesis tests carried out with only two variables, are seldom used as the primary means of hypothesis testing in political science research today. But it is imperative to understand the basic mechanics of bivariate hypothesis tests before moving to more complicated tests. This same logic applies to the use of statistical computing software. In this chapter, we teach you how to conduct hypothesis tests in SPSS using the three techniques presented in Chapter 8 of *FPSR*: tabular analysis, difference of means, and the correlation coefficient.

8.2 TABULAR ANALYSIS

In tabular analysis, we are testing the null hypothesis that the column variable and row variable are unrelated to each other. We will review the basics of producing a table in which the rows and columns are defined by the values of two different variables, generating hypothesis-testing statistics, and then presenting what you have found. We will learn to do this using the data sets from the main text, which include the 2016 American National Election Study – a survey of public opinion taken during that year's presidential campaign.

As is our practice, the data are located in the directory "C:\MyFPSRSPSSFiles" on the computer that created this workbook. To navigate to that folder, we use the pull-down menus – "File" then "Open" then "Data" – and then change the drive and directory as necessary until we find the correct location where the data set is stored. The data file is called "ANES2016small.sav." Once you've found it, open it.[1]

We produce a tabular analysis in SPSS by using the Crosstabs command, which we run by using the pull-down menu by clicking "Analyze," then "Descriptive Statistics," then "Crosstabs...." That process is shown in Figure 8.1.

That will open a dialog box where we will choose which variables from the data set to analyze, shown in Figure 8.2. In that figure, you can see the list of variables available in the data set from which you can choose, and selection boxes for which variables we want in the rows and columns. As we note in Chapter 8 of *FPSR*, it is customary to

---

[1] A reminder: All of the data sets we use can be found in the SPSS directory at www.cambridge.org/fpsr.

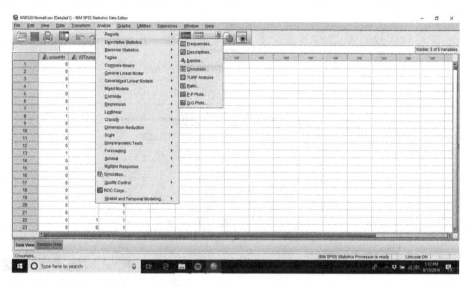

Figure 8.1 Navigating to SPSS's Crosstabs command

Figure 8.2 The dialog box for SPSS's Crosstabs command

put your dependent variable into the "Row(s)" box and your independent variable into the "Column(s)" box.

As detailed in Chapter 8 of *FPSR*, if we set up our independent and dependent variables like this, then column percentages allow for the comparison of interest – they tell us how the dependent variable values differ in terms of their distribution across values of the independent variable. It is crucial, when working with tables of this nature, to put the appropriate variables across the rows and columns of the table and then to present the column frequencies. (If you need a refresher on this, look at the tables in Figure 8.5 of the main text.)

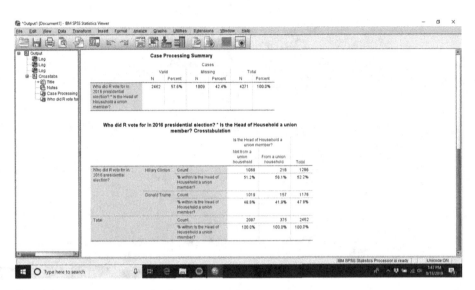

Figure 8.3 Raw output from SPSS's Crosstabs command

For example, if we were to attempt to recreate Table 8.2 in *FPSR*, we would click on "unionHH" in the variables list in the left-hand box, and click the arrow to place that variable into the "Column(s)" box, then click on "V2Trump" and click the arrow to place that variable into the "Row(s)" box – where "V2Trump" is a categorical variable that takes on a value of "1" if the respondent reported voting for Donald Trump and "0" if the respondent reported voting for Hillary Clinton, and "unionHH" is a variable that takes on a value of "1" if the respondent reported that someone in their household belonged to a union and "0" otherwise. In order to obtain column percentages, we click on the "Cells…" box on the right-hand side of the dialog box, and under "Percentages," check "Column." Then click "Continue" and then "OK" at the bottom of the Crosstabs dialog box. The output from this running command is displayed in Figure 8.3. Take a moment to compare this raw output with Table 8.2 in *FPSR*. There are two notable differences. First, in order to isolate the numbers needed for the assessment at hand (whether or not voters from union households voted differently from voters from nonunion households in the 2016 election), in Table 8.2 of the main text we only present the column percentages. Second, in the table in the main text, we have added a note making it clear what are the values reported in each cell of the table.

A note of caution: In the "Cells…" box, you'll notice that there are a *lot* of choices. What would happen if – say, because you happened to forget which type of information you want in your cells – you checked them all? The resulting table would be a frightening mess, containing way too much information, which would obscure the actual pattern you sought to discover. Just for fun, you can go ahead and try it. You'll see.

8.2.1   Generating Test Statistics

In Chapter 8 of *FPSR* we discuss in detail the logic of Pearson's chi-squared test statistic which we use to test the null hypothesis that the row and column variables are not related. To get this test statistic and the associated *p*-value for a two-variable table in

Figure 8.4 Obtaining the Chi-square statistic from SPSS's Crosstabs command

SPSS, from the Crosstabs dialog box, we click the "Statistics..." box on the far right, and then check the "Chi-square" box in the top-left of that new dialog box, and then click "Continue" (and "OK" to run the tabular analysis again).

That output is displayed in Figure 8.4. The calculated value of the Chi-square statistic is 6.171 – you could do it by hand following the formula in Chapter 8 of the main text – and the associated p-value is 0.013. Because that is less than 0.05, the relationship is statistically significant, meaning we are at least 95 percent confident – actually, 98.7 percent confident, to be precise – that the relationship we observe in our sample did not occur because of chance, and exists in the underlying population.

8.2.2 Putting Tabular Results into Papers

We recommend that you make your own tables in whatever word processing program you choose to use instead of copying and pasting the tables that you make in SPSS. The first reason for doing so is that you will think about your results more closely when you are producing your own tables. This will help you to catch any mistakes that you might have made and to write more effectively about what you have found. Another reason for doing so is that tables constructed by you will tend to look better. (By comparison, look at all of the clutter in the Chi-square test shown in Figure 8.4. Who wants all of that in their assignments, papers, and presentations?) By controlling how the tables are constructed, you will be able to communicate with maximum clarity.

As a part of making your own tables, you should have the goal in mind that your table communicates something on its own. In other words, if someone *only* looked at your table, would they be able to figure out what was going on? If the answer is "yes," then you have constructed an effective table. We offer the following advice ideas for making useful tables:

- Give your table a title that conveys the essential result in your table
- Make your column and row headings as clear as possible
- Put notes at the bottom of your table to explain the table's contents

8.3   DIFFERENCE OF MEANS

As we show in Table 8.1 in the main text, difference of means tests are conducted when we have a continuous dependent variable and a categorical independent variable.

8.3.1   Examining Differences Graphically

When we use graphs to assess a difference of means, we are graphing the distribution of the continuous dependent variable for two or more values of the limited independent variable. Figure 8.1 of *FPSR* shows how this is done with a box–whisker plot, which we learned to do in SPSS in Chapter 6 of this workbook. We will learn to do this using the data sets from the main text, which include the data set on government duration.

As is our practice, the data are located in the directory "C:\MyFPSRSPSSFiles" on the computer that created this workbook. To navigate to that folder, we use the pull-down menus – "File" then "Open" then "Data" – and then change the drive and directory as necessary until we find the correct location where the data set is stored. The data file is called "govts.sav." Once you've found it, open it.

As a reminder of what we learned in Chapter 6, we make the box–whisker plot using SPSS's Chart Builder. We begin by using the pull-down menu and selecting "Graphs" followed by "Chart Builder...." That opens up the Chart Builder dialog box, and from there, we begin in the lower-left portion, and click on "Boxplot" from the "Gallery" tab. Then double-click "Simple Boxplot," which activates the chart preview in the pane above. From the variable list in the top-left, grab and drag "Number of days in government" onto the *y* (vertical) axis of the chart preview area, and grab and drag the variable "Is the government a minority government?" onto the *x* (horizontal) axis. Then click "OK" to see our box–whisker plot.

Figure 8.5 displays our resulting boxplot, and it's quite similar to Figure 8.1 in the main text. As we learned in Chapter 6, it's easy to edit these graphs to add or remove details to or from our axes, for example.

8.3.2   Generating Test Statistics

To conduct a difference of means *t*-test such as the one discussed in Chapter 8 of *FPSR*, we navigate through the pull-down menus by clicking "Analyze," then "Compare Means," then "Independent-Samples T Test...," which opens up a dialog box like the one pictured in Figure 8.6. Our dependent variable, which must be continuous, is the "Number of days in government?" variable, so we click that from our variable list on the left and use the arrow key to insert it into the "Test Variable(s)" box. Our independent variable is the variable "Is the government a minority government?" variable, so we click that into the "Grouping Variable" box using the arrow. We then have to define the groups, so click on the "Define Groups..." button, which opens another dialog box. Our values for that variable are 0 and 1, so type those (respectively) into the boxes for Group 1 and Group 2, then click "Continue," and then "OK" to run the analysis.

The output appears in Figure 8.7. You will note there that it provides all of the means and standard deviations that appear in Table 8.11 of the main text, followed by the *t*-test

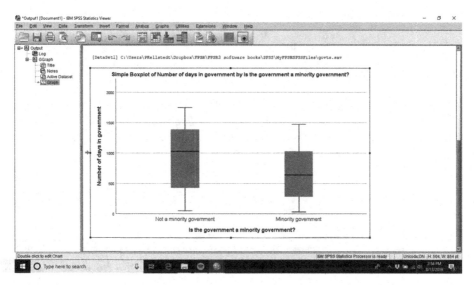

Figure 8.5 A boxplot of the lengths of majority and minority governments

Figure 8.6 The independent *t*-test dialog box menu in SPSS

calculation. The calculated $t = 3.443$, and you'll see on page 177 of *FPSR* that our calculated $t = 3.44$.

8.4   CORRELATION COEFFICIENTS

Correlation coefficients summarize the relationship between two continuous variables. They are also an important building block to understanding the basic mechanics of two-variable regression models.

To practice calculating correlation coefficients, let's use the data set on economic voting created by Ray Fair. As always, the data are located in the directory

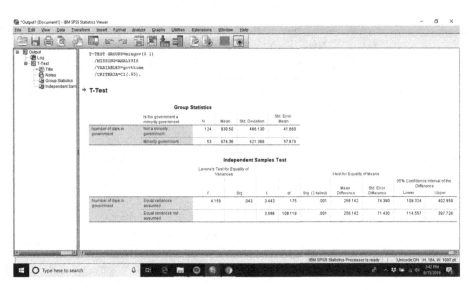

Figure 8.7 Output from the independent t-test

"C:\MyFPSRSPSSFiles" on the computer that created this workbook. To navigate to that folder, we use the pull-down menus – "File" then "Open" then "Data" – and then change the drive and directory as necessary until we find the correct location where the data set is stored. The data file is called "FairFPSR3.sav." Once you've found it, open it.

8.4.1   Producing Scatter Plots

We can examine the relationship between two continuous variables in a scatter plot such as Figure 8.3 in *FPSR*, which displays the relationship between economic growth and vote percentages for the incumbent party in US presidential elections.

We make the scatter plot using SPSS's Chart Builder. We begin by using the pull-down menu and selecting "Graphs" followed by "Chart Builder...." That opens up the Chart Builder dialog box, and from there, we begin in the lower-left portion, and click on "Scatter/Dot" from the "Gallery" tab. Then double-click "Simple Scatter," which activates the chart preview in the pane above. From the variable list in the top-left, grab and drag "inc_vote" onto the y (vertical) axis of the chart preview area, and grab and drag the variable "growth" onto the x (horizontal) axis. Then click "OK" to see our scatter plot.

The result is displayed in Figure 8.8, and you'll see a striking resemblance between that and Figure 8.3 in the main text. As before, there might be details that we'd like to edit for purposes of turning in assignments, writing papers, or making presentations – especially about titles and axis labels. You can edit those by double-clicking on the graph in the output window and editing away, as we showed you in Chapter 2 of this workbook.

8.4.2   Generating Correlation Coefficients and Test Statistics

To obtain a correlation coefficient like the one on page 183 of *FPSR*, we use the pull-down menu and click "Analyze," then "Correlate," then "Bivariate...," which will open up a simple dialog box. We simply click the variables there for which we want to

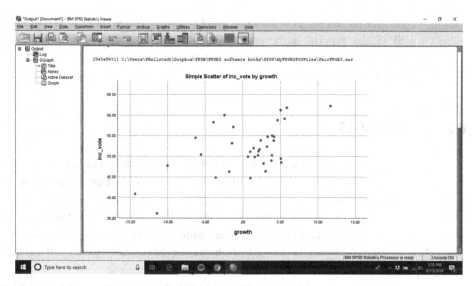

Figure 8.8 Output from a scatter plot

Figure 8.9 Output from the SPSS Correlate command

produce the correlations, and use the right arrow to add them to the "Variables" window on the right-hand side.[2] You'll see that the "Pearson" box is checked by default – if it is not, go ahead and check it – and then click "OK."

The output is displayed in Figure 8.9. You'll see that SPSS produces a correlation matrix, which shows the correlations across all pairs of variables. So, for example, "inc_vote" correlates at exactly 1 with itself, and the same is true of "growth." (Hopefully, that's intuitive.) The correlation between "inc_vote" and "growth" is 0.569, which

---

[2] If we would like to compute the covariance table like Table 8.13 in the main text, that can be checked under "Options."

(except for rounding) is the same number we calculated on page 183 of the main text. SPSS also reports, in the row "Sig. (2-tailed)," that the p-value for this correlation coefficient is 0.000, which means that the relationship is statistically significant at (at least) the 0.001 level.

8.5   EXERCISES

1.   Launch SPSS and open the "ANES2016small.sav" data set. Once you have done this, run the code to produce the example output presented in Section 8.2 of this book.

(a)   Calculate a chi-squared test for the output presented in Figure 8.4. Report the results of this test and write about what it tells you about the theory that voters in union households are more likely to support candidates from the left.

(b)   A commonly expressed theory of politics is that people who are dissatisfied with the performance of the legislature are more likely to vote for candidates who are political outsiders. Test this theory with a hypothesis test using the variables "StronglyDisapproveCongress" (coded as "1" if the respondent reported that they strongly disapprove of the way that Congress was doing its job) and "V2Trump." Produce an appropriate table to show what you have found and report the results from a chi-squared test for the hypothesis test. Write about what this analysis tells you about the theory in question.

2.   Launch SPSS and open the "govts.sav" data set.

(a)   Once you have done this, run the code to produce Figures 8.1 and 8.2 from *FPSR*. Copy and paste these figures into your word processing document.

(b)   A commonly expressed theory of politics is that governments which contain the party which got the most votes at the last election have more of an electoral mandate and thus will last longer. Test this theory with a hypothesis test using the variables "eptyplur" (coded as "1" if the party which received the most votes was in the government and "0" otherwise) and "govttime." Produce appropriate figures and a table to show what you have found and report the results from a t-test for the hypothesis test. Write about what this analysis tells you about the theory in question.

3.   Launch SPSS and open the "FairFPSR3.sav" data set.

(a)   Once you have done this, run the code to produce Figure 8.3 from *FPSR*. Copy and paste this figure into your word processing document.

(b)   As we discuss in *FPSR*, there are many different ways to measure economic performance, the independent variable in the theory of economic voting. Go through the steps that we go through in the lab, but replace the variable "growth" with "inflation." Produce an appropriate figure and a table to show what you have found and report the results from a t-test for the hypothesis test on the correlation coefficient. Write about what this analysis tells you about the theory of economic voting.

9 TWO-VARIABLE REGRESSION MODELS

9.1 OVERVIEW

In Chapter 9 of *FPSR* we introduce the two-variable regression model. As we discuss, this is another two-variable hypothesis test that amounts to fitting a line through a scatter plot of observations on a dependent variable and an independent variable. In this chapter, we walk you through how to estimate such a bivariate model in SPSS.

9.2 ESTIMATING A TWO-VARIABLE REGRESSION

The estimation of a two-variable regression model in SPSS, as discussed in Chapter 9 of *FPSR*, is fairly straightforward. To practice, let's use the data set on economic voting created by Ray Fair. As always, the data are located in the directory "C:\MyFPSRSPSSFiles" on the computer that created this workbook. To navigate to that folder, we use the pull-down menus – "File" then "Open" then "Data" – and then change the drive and directory as necessary until we find the correct location where the data set is stored. The data file is called "FairFPSR3.sav." Once you've found it, open it.[1]

In SPSS, we perform a regression analysis using the pull-down menu through clicking "Analyze," then "Regression," then "Linear...." That will open a dialog box where we will choose which variables from the data set to analyze. A screenshot of that dialog box appears in Figure 9.1. The list of available variables to analyze are on the left part of the dialog box. Hover your mouse over those variables to see their descriptions. In order to perform the regression described in Section 9.3 of the main text – with incumbent vote percentage as the dependent variable, and economic growth as the independent variable – we select "inc_vote" from the list on the left, then click on the arrow to insert it in the "Dependent" box, and then click "growth" from the list on the left, and use the arrow to add it to the box of "Independent(s)." Then we click "OK."

A portion of the results from the output window appears in Figure 9.2. We say "a portion," because it's rather hard to deny that SPSS provides a rather heavy dose of information in its regression output. Near the bottom of the figure, in the portion

---

[1] Again, all of the data sets we use can be found in the SPSS directory at www.cambridge.org/fpsr.

Figure 9.1 The linear regression dialog box in SPSS

Figure 9.2 Bivariate regression output in SPSS

labeled "Coefficients," you'll see the slope and Y-intercept that we estimated. Of greatest interest to us is the row labeled "growth," as this shows the relationship between the independent variable (GDP growth) and our dependent variable (incumbent vote percentage). In the column labeled "B," you'll see that the coefficient there is reported as 0.625. The row just above that, labeled "(Constant)," gives us the Y-intercept; in the column labeled "B," you'll see that the Y-intercept is 51.449. Altogether, that means that the formula for our regression line is $Y = 51.449 + 0.625X$ – which (save for the number of digits provided) is exactly equal to the reported regression line at the very top of page 195 of the main text.

The next column over from column B in the coefficients is labeled "Std. Error" – for "standard error" – as described in Section 9.4.4 of the main text. The t-test calculated on page 203 of the main text can be replicated by looking at the output. When looking at the SPSS output, the coefficient (0.625) divided by its standard error (0.155) equals the calculated t-statistic (reported in the column "t" in the table) of 4.032. Note that (again, save for the number of digits displayed) that is the same as the calculated t on page 203 of *FPSR*. The last column of the SPSS output, labeled "Sig.," provides the exact p-value. In this case, the value reported there – 0.000 – might be somewhat confusing. Because SPSS only provides three digits there, the best way to read that p-value is that it is "less than 0.001," or, equivalently, that the relationship between growth and incumbent vote share is statistically significant at the 0.001 level.

SPSS provides other pieces of information that are of interest to us as well. The root mean-squared error described in Section 9.4.1 of the main text can be seen in Figure 9.2 under the "Model Summary" portion near the top. It is in the column "Std. Error of the Estimate," which is another name for the root mean-squared error. The value there is 4.82817. That same portion of the output also shows the R-squared (or R^2) statistic, in the column labeled "R Square." The value there is 0.323.

9.3   GRAPHING A TWO-VARIABLE REGRESSION

To better understand what is going on in a two-variable regression model, it is often helpful to graph the regression line. An example of this is presented in Figure 9.4 of *FPSR*. We can produce a figure nearly identical to that by using SPSS's Chart Builder. Follow the procedures outlined in Chapter 8 of this workbook to produce a scatter plot, but instead of choosing the "Simple Scatter" from the "Gallery" menu, choose

Figure 9.3 Graphing the regression line in SPSS

Figure 9.4 Output of a scatter plot with a regression line in SPSS

the "Simple Scatter with Fit Line" option. In Figure 9.3, the mouse is hovered above that option. Then choose the variables as you did in Chapter 8, and click "OK."

The results are displayed in Figure 9.4, which looks very similar to Figure 9.4 in the main text. By now, you're perhaps used to our small quibbles about the default chart title and axis labels. You can (and should!) double-click the chart to edit those to make more meaningful labels.

9.4   EXERCISES

1.   Launch SPSS and open the "FairFPSR3.sav" data set. Once you have done this, use the Chart Builder to produce, as closely as possible, Figure 9.4 from *FPSR*. Copy and paste this figure into your word processing document.

2.   If we change the independent variable from our running example from "growth" to "inflation," what would the theory of economic voting lead us to expect in terms of a hypothesis for the slope of a regression line with variable "inc_vote" as the dependent variable and "inflation" as the independent variable? Explain your answer.

3.   Estimate a regression model with the variable "inc_vote" as the dependent variable and "inflation" as the independent variable.

   (a)   Copy and paste this output into your word processing document.

   (b)   Write about the results from the hypothesis test that you discussed above. What does this tell you about the theory of economic voting?

   (c)   Produce a figure like Figure 9.4 from *FPSR* but with inflation as the independent variable (inc_vote should remain as the dependent variable). Copy and paste this figure into your word processing document.

10 MULTIPLE REGRESSION: THE BASICS

10.1 OVERVIEW

In Chapter 10 of *FPSR*, we introduce the multiple regression model in which we are able to estimate the effect of X on Y holding Z constant. Here, we show you how to execute such models in SPSS.

10.2 ESTIMATING A MULTIPLE REGRESSION

The estimation of a multiple regression model, as discussed in Chapters 10 and 11 of *FPSR*, is just an extension of the command used for estimating a two-variable regression. To practice, we'll continue to use the data set on economic voting created by Ray Fair. As always, the data are located in the directory "C:\MyFPSRSPSSFiles" on the computer that created this workbook. To navigate to that folder, we use the pull-down menus – "File" then "Open" then "Data" – and then change the drive and directory as necessary until we find the correct location where the data set is stored. The data file is called "FairFPSR3.sav." Once you've found it, open it.[1]

In SPSS, we perform a multiple regression analysis using the pull-down menu through clicking "Analyze," then "Regression," then "Linear...." That will open the familiar dialog box from Chapter 9 of this workbook, where we will choose which variables from the data set to analyze. A screenshot of that dialog box appears in Figure 9.1. The list of available variables to analyze are on the left part of the dialog box. Hover your mouse over those variables to see their descriptions. In order to estimate the multiple regression displayed under the column C in Table 10.1 of *FPSR* – with incumbent vote percentage as the dependent variable, and with economic growth and the number of consecutive quarters of good news about the economy as the two independent variables – we select "inc_vote" from the list on the left, then click on the arrow to insert it in the "Dependent" box, and then click "growth" from the list on the left, and use the arrow to add it to the box of "Independent(s)," and also click

---

[1] Again, all of the data sets we use can be found in the SPSS directory at www.cambridge.org/fpsr.

Figure 10.1 Multiple regression output in SPSS

"goodnews" from the list on the left and add that, also, to the box of "Independent(s)."[2] Then click "OK."[3]

Figure 10.1 shows a portion of the SPSS output. Compare it to column C in Table 10.1 of *FPSR*. As before, there is the small difference between the number of digits past the decimal point presented. Otherwise, we trust that you find them to be identical. Interpreting the output is done in the same way as in Chapter 9 of this workbook and Chapter 10 of the main text.

10.3   FROM REGRESSION OUTPUT TO TABLE – MAKING ONLY ONE TYPE OF COMPARISON

As we discuss in Section 10.9 of *FPSR*, when presenting the results from more than two regression models in the same table, it is important that we set up our comparisons appropriately – either as comparisons of different model specifications estimated with the same sample of data, or as the same model specification estimated with different samples of data. This is because if both the sample of data and the model specification change, then we cannot know for sure whether any differences in the estimates that we are observing are due to the different sample or the different specification.

---

[2] The order in which the independent variables appear does not matter; you will get the same results regardless of their order.

[3] In practice, you may have as many independent variables as you want in a regression model as long as you meet the minimum mathematical requirements that each independent variable must vary, $n > k$, and you have no perfect multicollinearity. The first two of these requirements are discussed in Section 9.5 and the third is discussed in Section 10.7.1 of *FPSR*.

10.3.1   Comparing Models with the Same Sample of Data, but Different Specifications

If your data set doesn't have any missing values for any of the variables that you want to include in a set of models with different specifications, then making a table for such comparisons is pretty straightforward. All that you need to do is estimate the regressions of interest to you, and then put them into separate columns of a table. But if, as is often the case, you have some missing values for some of the variables that you are including in your different models, then you need to take some extra steps in order to make sure that the regressions that you are comparing are all estimated with the exact same observations.

As an example of this, we will use the regressions that were used to produce the results presented in Table 10.1 of *FPSR*. If you compare the output presented in Figure 10.1 with that presented in Figure 9.5 of *FPSR*, one thing that you might notice is that the regression presented in Figure 9.5 of *FPSR* has 36 observations, whereas the regression presented in Figure 10.1 has 35. This is the case because the variable "goodnews" is missing for the 1876 election. Thus, to obtain the output presented in Table 10.1 of *FPSR*, it is necessary to exclude the observation for 1876 from the model that we estimate to produce the results presented in column A of Table 10.1 of *FPSR*.

Given that we know the year of the observation that we want to exclude, we can simply tell SPSS to select all cases where the value of the variable "year" is greater than 1876. We do this by clicking on "Data," then "Select Cases...," which opens up a dialog box. This is displayed in Figure 10.2. From this point, we choose the radio button "If condition is satisfied," and click the "If..." button, which opens yet another dialog box.

We now have to tell SPSS which criteria to use to select cases. You could, at this point, click on variable names and use the keypad in the dialog box, as displayed in Figure 10.3, but you can also just click in the white box at the top of that dialog box and type "year > 1876" and click "Continue," and then "OK." Then, if we went back

Figure 10.2 Selecting cases in SPSS

Figure 10.3 Specifying the criteria for selecting cases in SPSS

and re-ran the bivariate regression of incumbent vote percentage and economic growth that we learned in Chapter 9, we would have the results (on 35 cases, instead of 36) in column A of Table 10.1 of the main text.

It is important to remember one thing at this point: Unless you manually go back in the "Data" and "Select Cases…" menu to click on the "All cases" radio button at the top, SPSS will perform all subsequent analyses on the restricted sample of data. It's an easy thing to forget, so please be mindful of this feature.

It is worth reiterating that the procedure above only works when we know which variables are missing which observations. But what would we do if we didn't know exactly which observations are missing particular values of particular independent variables?[4] One of the easiest ways is just to estimate the model using all cases that are not missing for any of the independent variables that you plan to include in the models that you want to present. In our running example, we would need to click "Data," then "Select Cases…," then "If condition is satisfied," and click the "If…" button, which opens the familiar dialog box. Then we would type the following in the white command box at the top:

NOT(SYSMIS(inflation)|SYSMIS(goodnews))

and click "Continue" and "OK." From that point forward, our analyses would only be on non-missing cases for "goodnews" and "inflation," which would create the output presented in the various columns of Table 10.1.

And again, remember: Unless you manually go back in the "Data" and "Select Cases…" menu to click on the "All cases" radio button at the top, SPSS will perform all subsequent analyses on the restricted sample of data.

---

[4] If an observation is missing for the dependent variable, it will not be included in any of the models that we estimate. Also, in general, we should have gotten to know our data before we estimate a regression model, and part of getting to know one's data is figuring out what are the missing values and why they are missing.

10.3.2   Comparing Models with the Same Specification, but Different Samples of Data

As an example of how to compare models with the same specification, but different samples of data, let's imagine that we want to look at the results from our running example of economic voting in the United States for the observations after World War II compared with all observations before then. Although there are some different interpretations of when the war started, most people agree that World War II ended in 1945. So, to estimate models on samples of data after the war and all other cases, we would need to click "Data," "Select Cases…," "If condition is satisfied," and the "If…" button, which opens yet again the familiar dialog box. Then we would type "year > 1945" in the top box, click "Continue" and "OK," and run the regression model we want.

Then we would have to repeat the process, only this time substituting "year < 1945" into the top box, and re-run the regression model.

10.4   STANDARDIZED COEFFICIENTS

You may have noticed that SPSS automatically includes standardized coefficients in its multiple regression output. So, if you look again at Figure 10.1, under the "Coefficients" section, you'll see a column labeled "Standardized Coefficients Beta." The values in that column are identical (save for the number of digits past the decimal points) to those computed on page 226 of the main text.

10.5   EXERCISES

1.   Launch SPSS and open the "FairFPSR3.sav" data set. Once you have done this, run the commands to produce the output shown in Figure 10.1. Copy and paste this figure into your word processing document.

2.   Estimate a multiple regression model with both inflation and growth as the independent variables and inc_vote as the dependent variable. Estimate the two two-variable models needed to make a table like Table 10.1 of *FPSR* where you are comparing the results across three specifications on the same sample of observations. Put your results into a table in your word processing document and write about what you have found.

3.   Estimate the two multiple regression models described in this chapter with the same specification but where the sample is divided according to whether the observation occurred before or after 1945. Put these results into a table in your word processing document and write about what you have found.

4.   Estimate a multiple regression model with standardized coefficients with goodnews, inflation, and growth as the independent variables, and inc_vote as the dependent variable. Put your results into a table in your word processing document and write about what you have found.

11 MULTIPLE REGRESSION MODEL SPECIFICATION

11.1 OVERVIEW

In Chapter 11 of *FPSR* we discuss a series of issues that researchers commonly encounter when they are trying to test their theories using multiple regression models. In this chapter, we show SPSS procedures for how to proceed when one encounters these issues.

11.2 DUMMY VARIABLES

As we discuss in Section 11.2 of *FPSR*, dummy variables are categorical variables that take on one of two different values. The vast majority of the time in political science, these two values are "zero" and "one." Dummy variables are usually created and named so that "one" represents the presence of a condition and "zero" represents the absence of that condition. In order not to confuse the people who will be reading your work or watching your presentations, it is a good idea to follow these conventions. For example, if you have a dummy variable to identify the gender identity of a survey respondent, it might be tempting to call the variable "gender." That, however, would leave unclear the issue of what the zeros and ones represent. If, by contrast, you named your variable "female," then the convention would be that a zero is for male respondents – or the absence of the condition "female" – and one is for the female respondents – the presence of the condition "female."

11.2.1 Creating a Dummy Variable in SPSS

Sometimes data sets that you are working with come with proper dummy variables already created for you. When they do not, you will need to create your own variables. There are multiple ways to create dummy variables in SPSS. In the "Transform" pull-down menu, there are two options that might seem like they serve the same function: "Recode into Same Variables…" and "Recode into Different Variables…." We strongly urge you to always use the "Recode into Different Variables…" option, as it greatly reduces the possibilities of you making a costly and irreversible mistake. We will learn to do this using the data sets from the main text, which include the 1996 American

Figure 11.1 Creating a new dummy variable in SPSS

National Election Study – a survey of public opinion taken during that year's presidential campaign.

As is our practice, the data are located in the directory "C:\MyFPSRSPSSFiles" on the computer that created this workbook. To navigate to that folder, we use the pull-down menus – "File" then "Open" then "Data" – and then change the drive and directory as necessary until we find the correct location where the data set is stored. The data file is called "ANES1996small.sav." Once you've found it, open it.[1]

From the codebook for this study, we can tell that coding of values for each respondent's self-identified gender is in the variable named "v960066," and that the values of this variable are equal to 1 for "male" and 2 for "female." To check the values for this variable, let's look at a frequency distribution, as we learned in Chapter 6 of this workbook. Having seen that there are only values equal to 1 and 2 (and no others that we have to worry about or account for), we can now create the variable "female" and check what we have created using the "Recode into Different Variables..." command.

So click "Transform" on the pull-down menu, then "Recode into Different Variables...," which will open a dialog box like the one you see in Figure 11.1. The first step is to pick the original variable, which is "v960066," from the list on the left-hand side, and use the blue arrow button to select it into the "Input Variable –> Output Variable" window. Next, on the far right-hand side of the dialog box, the "Output Variable" box will become active. We can type "female" in the "Name" box and "Gender of respondent" in the "Label" box. We then have to click the "Change" button just below those boxes.

Our next step is to click on the "Old and New Values..." button, which opens up another embedded dialog box, as shown in Figure 11.2. Recall from above that, in

---

[1] A reminder: All of the data sets we use can be found in the SPSS directory at www.cambridge.org/fpsr.

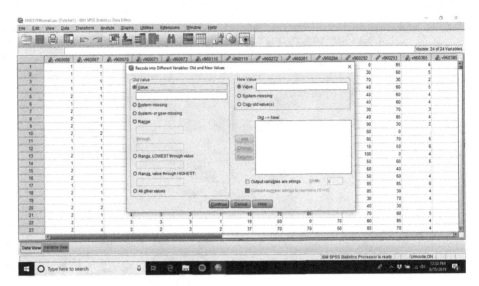

Figure 11.2 Recoding old and new values in SPSS

v960066, males are coded 1, but in our new variable "female," we will have them coded as 0. So in the "Old Value" portion of the new dialog box, we type 1 in the space marked "Value," and in the "New Value" portion, we type 0 in the space labeled "Value." Then, just below, click the "Add" button. Next, we need to recode the female respondents from 2 in v960066 to 1 in our "female" variable, so type 2 in the "Old Value" window and 1 in the "New Value" window, and click "Add" again.[2] Then click "Continue" and "OK." Voilà. You've just created a new dummy variable.

Whenever you create a new variable, it is critically important to check that you created exactly what you intended to create. In this case, we could check our work with a tabular analysis, which (if we have done our work correctly) would show a perfect relationship between the old and new variables. So let's do that, and run a tabular analysis using the "Analyze," "Descriptive Statistics," and "Crosstabs…" selections from the pull-down menu. We would then need to put v960066 and "female" into our rows and columns – it doesn't matter which one you put where – and click "OK." Doing so reveals that we have not misclassified any respondents.

11.2.2   Estimating a Multiple Regression Model with a Single Dummy Independent Variable

As we discussed in Section 11.2 of this workbook, the procedure for estimating a multiple regression with three independent variables is straightforward. We do this by using the pull-down menu through clicking "Analyze," then "Regression," then "Linear…." That will open the familiar dialog box from Chapter 9 of this workbook, where we will choose which variables from the data set to analyze. The list of available variables to analyze are on the left part of the dialog box. We select our dependent variable from the list on the left, then click on the arrow to insert it in the "Dependent" box, and then click

---

[2] Obviously, you can see from Figure 11.2 that there are lots of other options for recoding variables which may be of use to you in other circumstances.

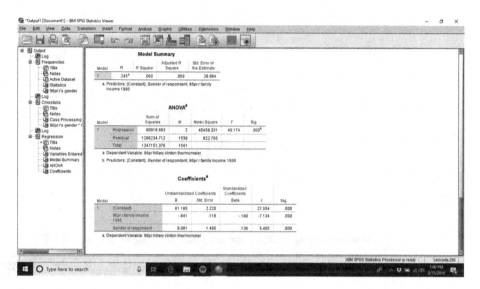

Figure 11.3 Output from a regression model with a dummy variable

whatever variables we want, one at a time, from the list on the left, and use the arrow to add them to the box of "Independent(s)."

As an example of this, we can estimate the regression model displayed on the left side of Table 11.1 of *FPSR* from the 1996 ANES by using the variable "v960281" as the dependent variable (respondents' thermometer ratings of Hillary Clinton), "v960701" as a continuous independent variable representing family income, and "female" as the dummy independent variable that we just created. Note that, as was the case with our multiple regression models with multiple continuous independent variables, the order of the independent variables does not matter for this command. The output from this command is displayed in Figure 11.3.

11.2.3   Estimating a Multiple Regression Model with Multiple Dummy Independent Variables

To estimate a multiple regression model with multiple dummy variables, you use the same procedure as in the previous section. The main complication comes when the multiple dummy variables represent values for a categorical variable with more than two values. As we discuss in Section 11.2.2 of *FPSR*, in such a case, in order to avoid what is known as the "dummy variable trap," you need to leave one category of such an independent variable out of the regression model, and that omitted category becomes the "reference category."

11.3   DUMMY VARIABLES IN INTERACTIONS

In Section 11.3 of *FPSR*, we discuss testing interactive hypotheses with dummy variables. There are several different ways to do this in SPSS. We recommend that you use a fairly straightforward approach where you start out by creating a new variable

Figure 11.4 Creating an interaction variable

that is the multiplicative interaction between the dummy independent variable and the continuous independent variable. We'll again follow along the example from that section of the main text.

In order to create the interactive model displayed on the right side of Table 11.6 of *FPSR*, we first create the interaction between the continuous variable "v961039" (which are the respondents' thermometer scores for the women's movement), and the dummy variable "female" with the following procedure. Under the "Transform" menu, click on "Compute Variable...." That will open a dialog box like the one shown in Figure 11.4. We need to give our new variable a name, so in the "Target Variable" box in the top-left, type "womenmvmt_thermo_female" (though, of course, you can name the variable anything). Beneath that box, click on the "Type & Label" box and type "Interaction of women's movement thermometer and gender" and then click "Continue."

Back in the main dialog box for computing variables, we then define the interaction in the "Numeric Expression" box in the upper right. So, using the variable list along the left-hand side, click to find "v961039" and use the blue arrow to select it into the "Numeric Expression" box. Then type "*" (for multiplication), and then use the variable list again to click on "female" and use the blue arrow to move it into the "Numeric Expression" box. Your screen should look like the screenshot in Figure 11.5. Then click "OK."

So, to create the interactive model displayed on the right side of Table 11.6 of *FPSR*, we simply run a linear regression model using the procedures we have already described, with the dependent variable being "v960281" (the respondents' thermometer ratings of Hillary Clinton), and our three independent variables being "v961039" (which are the respondents' thermometer scores for the women's movement), the dummy variable "female," and our interaction variable "womenmvmt_thermo_female." When you run that model, you should get output like that in Figure 11.6, which (you will see) contains the same results as the "Interactive model" column in Table 11.6 of the main text.

Figure 11.5 Details for creating an interaction variable

Figure 11.6 Output from a regression model with an interaction

11.4   POST-ESTIMATION DIAGNOSTICS IN SPSS FOR OLS

In Chapter 11 of *FPSR* we discuss a number of diagnostic procedures that can be carried out once an ordinary least-squares (OLS) model has been estimated. These procedures are all available in SPSS. It is important to keep in mind that, when asked to conduct such an analysis, SPSS will always do so using information from the most recent regression model that was estimated.

11.4.1   Identifying Outliers and Influential Cases in OLS

To identify outliers and influential cases in SPSS, we'll follow the example from Chapter 11 of the main text that focuses on the county-by-county Florida election results in 2000. As is our practice, the data are located in the directory "C:\MyFPSRSPSSFiles" on the computer that created this workbook. To navigate to that folder, we use the pull-down menus – "File" then "Open" then "Data" – and then change the drive and directory as necessary until we find the correct location where the data set is stored. The data file is called "florida2000.sav." Once you've found it, open it.

We can estimate the regression found in Table 11.7 of *FPSR* by using the "Analyze," "Regression," "Linear..." command, which opens the dialog box with which we've become familiar. The dependent variable in that table is the variable "BUCHANAN" (for the number of votes Pat Buchanan received in each county) and the independent variable is "GORE" (for the number of votes Al Gore received in each county).

We next click on the "Save..." button, which opens a new dialog box. We have checked several of the options there, as shown in Figure 11.7: "Unstandardized" Predicted Values, "Standardized" Residuals, "Leverage values," and "Standardized DfBeta(s)." Once you've done that, click "Continue" and then "OK" to run the model. You'll notice that the numbers in the "Coefficients" section match those presented in Table 11.7 of the main text (save for reporting different numbers of significant digits).

By checking those boxes in the "Save..." menu, SPSS created new variables in the data set. You can see them in the "Data View" if you scroll to the right of your main (not output) window, and see their descriptions in the "Variable View" tab. The column "SDB1_1" is the standardized DFBeta scores that are described on page 262 of the main text and presented in Table 11.8 on the same page. You can scroll up and down

Figure 11.7 Options on the "Save..." menu for quantities SPSS can generate after running a regression model

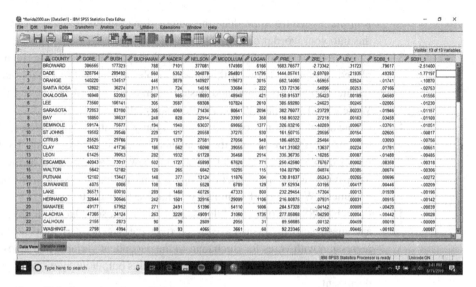

Figure 11.8 Screenshot of sorted DFBeta values

that column in Figure 11.8 to see that the numbers there match the values presented in Table 11.8 for those counties that had the greatest influence on our regression results in Table 11.7 of the main text. You might find it convenient to click on the title of that column, then right-click it, and select "Sort Ascending," which would sort the cases in order from lowest to highest, so make it easy to find extremely large negative (at the top) and extremely large positive (at the bottom) DFBeta scores. We've done just that in Figure 11.8, and you can see there the large negative values in the column "SDB1_1" for Broward, Dade, and Orange counties, and compare them to the numerical values in Table 11.8 of the main text.

11.4.2 Detecting Multicollinearity in OLS

As we discussed in Section 11.5 of *FPSR*, one way to detect multicollinearity is to estimate a variance inflation factor (or "VIF") for each independent variable after you have estimated your regression model. To get this information from SPSS, when specifying your regression model (in "Analyze," "Regression," "Linear...") select the "Statistics..." button and check the box marked "Collinearity diagnostics." SPSS will provide the VIF (described in Section 11.5.2 of the main text) for each independent variable on the far-right side of the "Coefficients" portion of the regression output.

11.5 EXERCISES

1. Launch SPSS and open the "ANES1996small.sav" data set. Once you have done this, run the procedure to produce the output shown in Figure 11.3. Copy and paste this into your word processing document.

2. Run the procedure to produce the output shown in Figure 11.6. Copy and paste this into your word processing document.

3. Create a dummy variable identifying male respondents. Estimate the model displayed in Figure 11.3 with this new variable instead of the variable identifying female respondents. Copy and paste this into your word processing document. Write a brief summary of what these results tell you.

4. Create an interaction between the new dummy variables that you created to identify male respondents and the women's movement thermometer. Estimate the model displayed in Figure 11.6 with this new variable instead of the variables identifying female respondents. Copy and paste this into your word processing document. Write a brief summary of what these results tell you.

5. Launch SPSS and open the "florida2000.sav" data set. Once you have done this and made sure that you have the correct data set loaded into SPSS, run the regression with votes for Buchanan as the dependent variable and votes for Gore as the independent variable. Copy and paste this output into your word processing document.

6. Run the procedures to produce the DFBETA scores that are presented in Table 11.8 of *FPSR*. In your word processing document, list the DFBETA values for the five counties with the smallest (in absolute values) scores for this calculation together with their DFBETA scores.

7. Launch SPSS and open the "ANES2004small.sav" data set. Estimate the model shown at the bottom of page 268 of the main text, and obtain VIF statistics for all of your independent variables. Copy and paste this output into your word processing document and write a brief summary of what these results tell you.

12 LIMITED DEPENDENT VARIABLES AND TIME-SERIES DATA

12.1 OVERVIEW

In Chapter 12 of *FPSR* we discuss two important extensions to multiple regression models: models with dichotomous dependent variables and models with time-series data. In this chapter we provide an explanation of the commands needed to deal with these circumstances in SPSS.

12.2 MODELS WITH DUMMY DEPENDENT VARIABLES

As we discuss in Chapter 12 of *FPSR*, there are several different models that can be used when we have a dummy dependent variable. We will learn to do this using the data sets from the main text, in this case the 2004 American National Election Study – a survey of public opinion taken during that year's presidential campaign.

As is our practice, the data are located in the directory "C:\MyFPSRSPSSFiles" on the computer that created this workbook. To navigate to that folder, we use the pull-down menus – "File" then "Open" then "Data" – and then change the drive and directory as necessary until we find the correct location where the data set is stored. The data file is called "ANES2004subset.sav." Once you've found it, open it.[1]

In this set of examples, we will work with a dependent variable named "Bush," which equals one for respondents who reported that they voted for George W. Bush and equals zero for those respondents who reported that they voted for John Kerry.[2] To get a look at the values for this variable, we can run a Frequencies command as we learned in Chapter 6 of this workbook.

Those values are displayed in Figure 12.1. As we discuss in Chapter 12 of *FPSR*, one option when we have a limited dependent variable is simply to run a linear regression model using the procedures that we discussed in Chapter 10 of this workbook ("Analyze," "Regression," "Linear..."). So, if we want to estimate the model displayed in Table 12.1 of *FPSR*, we would click the variable "Bush" into the "Dependent" box, and click (in any order) the variables "partyid," "eval_WoT," and "eval_HoE" – where

---

[1] A reminder: All of the data sets we use can be found in the SPSS directory at www.cambridge.org/fpsr.
[2] This is the same example that we use in Chapter 12 of *FPSR*. For a more detailed explanation of the variable and how it was created, see footnote 1 on page 274 of *FPSR*.

Figure 12.1 Frequency distribution for the variable "Bush"

"partyid" is "Party Identification," "eval_WoT" is "Evaluation: War on Terror," and "eval_HoE" is "Evaluation: Health of the Economy" – into the "Independent(s)" box. We would next need to click on the "Save…" box, and check the box under "Predicted Values" for "Unstandardized." Then click "Continue," and "OK."

To calculate and summarize the predicted probabilities from this model, we would run descriptive statistics like we learned in Chapter 6 of this workbook ("Analyze," "Descriptive Statistics," "Frequencies…") on the predicted values we just generated from our regression. That variable should be called "PRE_1" – though SPSS gives these variables names automatically. Once you've selected the variable, click the "Statistics…" button and select the options as in Figure 12.4 of this workbook, and click "Continue" and then "OK."

This will produce the output displayed in Figure 12.2. If we look at the results – scrolling down in your output below what is shown in Figure 12.2 – we can see that we get some predicted values that are greater than one. As we discuss in Chapter 12 of *FPSR*, one of the problems of the linear probability model is that it can produce predicted probabilities that are greater than one or less than zero. This is one of the main reasons why political scientists prefer to use either a binomial logit model or a binomial probit model when they have a dummy dependent variable.

To continue with our running example, we can produce the probit and logit columns of the results displayed in Table 12.2 of *FPSR* – respectively, the "BNP" column and the "BNL" column – and predicted probabilities for each observation by running the following procedures.

To estimate a binomial probit model in SPSS, we use the pull-down menu and select "Analyze," "Generalized Linear Models," and then again "Generalized Linear Models…," which opens a dialog box that is somewhat different from the linear

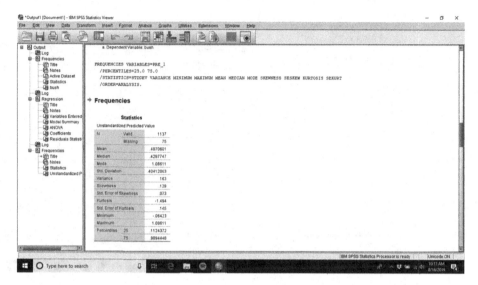

Figure 12.2 Calculating and displaying the predicted values from the linear probability model

Figure 12.3 The "Generalized Linear Models" menu, with the "Binary probit" radio button selected

regression dialog box.[3] That dialog box is shown in Figure 12.3. To run a binary probit model, we select the "Binary probit" radio button from the right-hand side of the "Type of Model" tab as displayed in the figure. To define our dependent variable, click on the "Response" tab at the top of the dialog box, and select your variable of interest and use the arrow key in the now-familiar way to click it into the "Dependent Variable" box.

By default, SPSS chooses the highest number as its reference category, but, by custom, most analysts choose the lowest value as the reference category. So click on the

---

[3] You might think that a probit model would be estimated by clicking on "Analyze," "Regression," "Probit...," but that leads to a different procedure.

Figure 12.4 Changing the reference category in a binary probit model

"Reference Category" button on the "Response" tab, and it will open another dialog box as displayed in Figure 12.4. Click on the "First (lowest value)" button and then click "Continue."

Next, click on the "Predictors" tab and, from the "Variables" list on the left, click your independent variables one by one (in any order) into the "Covariates" box. Next, click on the "Model" tab, and click all of your independent variables on the left (one at a time, in any order) and click the right arrow to move them all into the "Model" box on the right. Then click "OK" and you've run your model. The scrolled-down portion of the output is presented in Figure 12.5, and, as you'll see, those coefficients match the ones displayed in the "BNP" column in Table 12.2 of the main text.

To estimate a binomial logit model in SPSS, we have two options. We could follow the same procedure just described to estimate a binary probit model, except that, on the "Type of Model" tab displayed in Figure 12.3, we would select "Binary logistic" instead of "Binary probit." The rest of the procedure is identical. Alternatively and equivalently, we could use the pull-down menu and select "Analyze," "Regression," "Binary Logistic…," which opens a dialog box that looks and functions much like the now-familiar linear regression dialog box, with its space for the dependent variable and the independent variables (called "Covariates" here). The benefit of the latter procedure is that it makes it easy to obtain predicted probabilities, as discussed in the main text, by clicking on the "Save…" button and clicking the box marked "Probabilities" under the "Predicted Values" section (and then clicking "Continue").

To summarize the predicted probabilities from this model, we would run descriptive statistics like we learned in Chapter 6 of this workbook ("Analyze," "Descriptive Statistics," "Frequencies…") on the predicted values we just generated from our binomial logit. As before, SPSS gives these variables names automatically, so you'll have to search for predicted probabilities in your list of variables. Once you've selected the

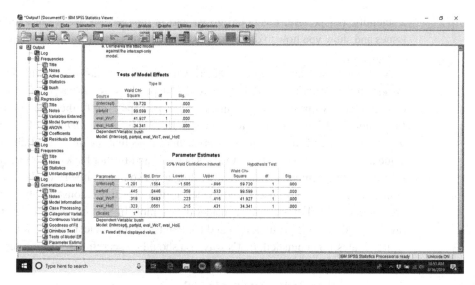

Figure 12.5 A portion of the output from a binary probit model

Figure 12.6 Displaying the predicted probabilities from the binary logit model

variable, click the "Statistics…" button and select the options as in Figure 12.4 of this workbook, and click "Continue" and then "OK." The output containing those predicted probabilities is displayed in Figure 12.6.

12.3   BEING CAREFUL WITH TIME-SERIES DATA

The section title here might seem a bit ominous. Why, after all, do we suggest that you need to "be careful" with time-series data? What could possibly go wrong? From a scientific perspective, lots could go wrong. In this section, we'll raise some crucial issues and show you how to draw the most appropriate conclusions from the time-series data you have.

All of the issues revolve around the critical issue of *dependence*, by which we simply mean that the value of a variable at any time t "depends" to some varying (but important) degree on its own past values: at time $t - 1$, or perhaps even further back in its history. In Section 12.3.2 of the main text, we described this as the *memory* of a series. The underlying principle at play in time-series analysis is that the more a variable's current value at time t depends on its past values at $t - 1$ (and further back), the more important it is to take the memory into account. Failing to do so makes it very likely – sometimes almost a certainty – to falsely find evidence of a causal relationship when one is not present in reality. (For example, consider the example in Section 12.3.3 of the main text involving golf course proliferation and the demise of the nuclear family in the post-war United States.) In a nutshell, that's why you should "be careful" with time series.

12.3.1   Setting Up a Time-Series Data Set in SPSS

This issue of dependence has lots of implications for how we should evaluate causal relationships involving time-series data. But it begins even before that. It has important (but simple) implications for how we set up a data set. To see why, consider a data set of cross-sectional data, where the cases are individual people responding to a survey. Typically, the individuals responding to a cross-sectional survey are selected randomly, which means that the presence of one individual from the underlying population does not affect the probability of another individual from the population being selected. That is, the selection of two different individual people from the population is *independent*. Picking one person doesn't affect the presence or absence of another person in the sample. As a result, when we consider the cases in our data set – the rows in the data file – the ordering of those rows doesn't matter. It makes no difference whether row 11 in our data file represents Friedrich from Frankfurt and row 12 represents Martina from Munich, or vice versa. Because the cases are presumed to be independent of one another, the ordering makes no difference whatsoever, and would have no effect on any statistical analyses we performed. That's not true in a time-series data set.

To see why, download the data set "Ch12TS.sav" from the *FPSR* website, and open it. Follow along on your own computer as we execute the following commands.

Because the observations contain the aforementioned dependence, the ordering of them in our data set matters. And SPSS will need to be told that the data set under consideration is a data set of ordered, time-series data. Figure 12.7 shows this for a data set of US President Bill Clinton's approval ratings over the 96 months of his two terms.

You'll notice in the data view that the first row of the data represents observations for the value of *Year* as 1993 and *Month* as 1. There is a system-generated variable called "DATE_" that has, in that first row, the value "JAN 1993." So that monthly observation, obviously, is for January of 1993, which is when President Clinton was inaugurated. Because the ordering of observations is important, yes, it matters that the first observation (row 1) in the data set is the first observation in the time series. Equally important is that the second row, as you can see from Figure 12.7, represents February

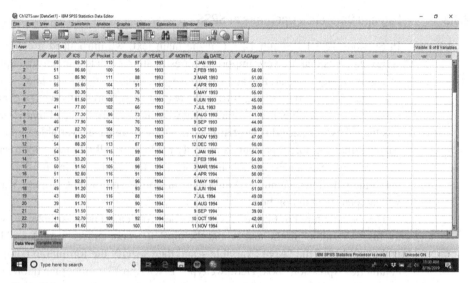

Figure 12.7 The data view of a time-series data set in SPSS

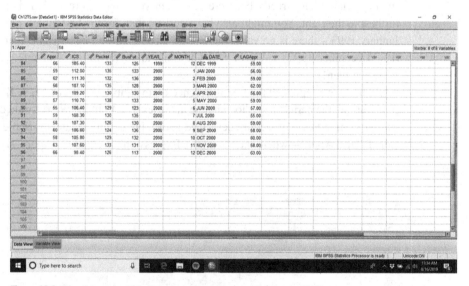

Figure 12.8 The data view of the last rows of a time-series data set in SPSS

of 1993. And so on. The 96th and final row of the data set, shown in Figure 12.8, is for December of 2000, President Clinton's last full month in office.[4] In short, the ordering of the observations in a time-series data set matters.

---

[4] The careful reader may have noticed that we used the word "full" in that sentence. President Clinton, of course, served until January 20, 2001. Thus it requires some care for the analyst to decide how to code polling observations from January 1–19, 2001. The same applies for the beginning of Clinton's first term, when George H.W. Bush was President for most of January 1993. In this case, we used only surveys in January 1993 after Clinton was inaugurated, and dropped any surveys in January 2001 before George W. Bush became President. The key point is not that you must do it this way, but that you must be careful and clear about such decisions.

12.3.2   Lag and Difference Operators in SPSS

In Sections 12.3.1 through 12.3.4 of the main text, we introduced a couple of time-series concepts that are very important for estimating models – in particular, the notion of *lagged* values of a variable and that of the *first difference* of a variable.

Lagged values, you will recall from the text, are just represented with a change in the subscripts of a variable. For a variable that we denote Y_t, the value of that variable when it is lagged by one period is written Y_{t-1}. In SPSS, if we have a variable "Appr" – in this data set, that variable represents a monthly reading of Bill Clinton's approval rating – then we can create a new variable that represents the one-period lag for that variable by using the pull-down menu, clicking on "Transform" and then "Compute Variable…," which opens up a dialog box.

That box, pictured in Figure 12.9, shows how to create a new variable. We first define a "Target Variable" in the text box at the top-left – here called "LAGAppr" because it is the first lag of the "Appr" variable – and then specify the formula to compute in the "Numeric Expression" box. Here, we type "LAG(Appr)" (without the quotes). Then we click "OK," and a new variable is created in the data set. Perhaps you've noticed that such a variable has already been created when you saw Figure 12.7. It is the column furthest to the right. You might also have noticed that, for the first month of the series – January 1993 – there is no value there. And there shouldn't be, because there is no lag (i.e., December 1992) value of Bill Clinton's approval rating available. (He wasn't President then!)

Similarly, we represent the first difference of a variable, Appr_t, as $\Delta Y_t = Y_t - Y_{t-1}$. So ΔY_t is simply the period-to-period change in the level of Y. In SPSS, we could do that in a similar fashion to the procedure described above, but simply create a variable – perhaps called "DIFFAppr" – where the "Numeric Expression" is equal to "Appr – LAGAppr."

Figure 12.9 Using the Compute command to create a lagged value of a variable

12.3.3   Performing Time-Series Regression Analyses in SPSS

Now that you know how to create time-series variables with lags and first differences, performing time-series regression analyses in SPSS is just as simple as all of the other regression analyses you already know in SPSS.

The data set that you should have open contains several other variables in addition to President Clinton's approval rating (the "Appr" variable). Of particular interest are three measures of consumer confidence, akin to what is described in Section 12.4 of the main text. The variable "ICS" is the Index of Consumer Sentiment, produced by the University of Michigan.[5] The five components of the "ICS" include measures of the public's views of both the past and the future of the economy, as it pertains both to a person's own financial situation and also to the economy as a whole. The index also includes an item about whether or not now is a good time to make major household purchases. Two of the components of the index are included in that data set: the variable "Pocket" assesses the public's beliefs about how their personal financial situation compares today to that of a year ago.[6] And the variable "BusFut" measures the public's perceptions of whether business conditions in the country are likely to get better or worse in the next five years.[7]

If we were to run a Koyck lagged-dependent-variable regression model on the relationship between President Clinton's approval rating and the overall Index of Consumer Sentiment, as presented in Section 12.3.5 of the main text, it would be of the form

$$\text{Appr}_t = \lambda \text{Appr}_{t-1} + \alpha + \beta_0 \text{ICS}_t + v_t.$$

And in SPSS, we would do that just as we do any other multiple regression as you learned from Chapter 10.

The results of that command are presented in Figure 12.10. Recall from Section 12.3.5 of *FPSR* what each of the estimated coefficients represents. As you can see in the output in Figure 12.10, the coefficient of 0.180 by the variable "ICS" represents the *immediate* impact of a one-point shift in the ICS on President Clinton's approval rating. When consumer confidence improves by one point, that is associated with an increase in President Clinton's approval of about 0.180 points. In other words, it would take a shift of a bit more than five points in consumer confidence to translate into a one-point shift in approval.

Perhaps that effect seems a bit small to you, but remember, the 0.180 only represents the *immediate* impact of a shift in consumer confidence on approval. The Koyck model allows us to compute the *cumulative* impact, β, of a one-point shift in the independent variable using the formula

---

[5] Michigan's Survey of Consumers website is: www.sca.isr.umich.edu/.

[6] The exact question wording is: "Would you say that you (and your family living there) are better off or worse off financially than you were a year ago?" Response options are "better," "same," or "worse."

[7] The exact question wording is: "Looking ahead, which would you say is more likely? That in the country as a whole we'll have continuous good times during the next five years or so, or that we'll have periods of widespread unemployment or depression, or what?" The response options are "good times," "uncertain," or "bad times."

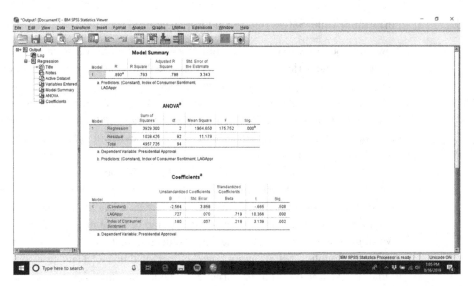

Figure 12.10 Output from a Koyck model in SPSS

$$\beta = \frac{\beta_0}{1 - \alpha}.$$

In this case, because $\alpha = 0.727$, this means that roughly 73 percent of a shift in the independent variable persists into the next period. Inserting this into the formula, we see that

$$\beta = \frac{0.180}{1 - 0.727} = \frac{0.180}{0.273} = 0.659.$$

The Koyck model, you recall, explicitly models the idea that shifts in the independent variable at time t might take a while – multiple periods of time – to realize their full effect. In other words, a shift in consumer confidence in March might take part of April or even May (or beyond) to fully be translated into an approval rating. This means that the *cumulative* – that is, added up over time – effect of a one-point shift in consumer confidence is roughly two-thirds of a point of approval. That's a good bit bigger than its immediate impact, as you can see.

We remind you of the lesson from Section 12.3.5 in the main text that the value of the coefficient for the lagged dependent variable – which represents the way that lagged values of the *independent* variable continue to have lingering effects on the dependent variable – should vary between 0 and 1. If the value is 0, then there are no lagged effects of the independent variable on the dependent variable, and the cumulative effect is simply the immediate impact. (You can see this from the algebra of the formula.) But the closer the value of the coefficient for the lagged dependent variable gets to 1, the more the quotient for the cumulative effect will grow.[8]

---

[8] Recall our admonition from the main text that if the coefficient for the lagged dependent variable equals or exceeds 1.0, this represents serious problems for our model.

12.4   EXERCISES

1. Launch SPSS and open the "FairFPSR3.sav" data set. Once you have done this, run the procedure to produce the results presented in Table 12.2 of *FPSR*. Copy and paste this table into your word processing document.

2. Calculate the proportionate reduction in error from a naive model to the BNL and from a naive model to the BNP. Write briefly about what you have learned from doing this.

3. Using the data set Ch12TS.sav, estimate a regression model of the effects of "ICS" on "Appr," without using a lagged dependent variable in the model. Answer the following questions:

   (a) What does the output tell you about the effects of a one-point shift in consumer confidence on President Clinton's approval ratings?

   (b) Examining the SPSS output, how well does the model fit the data? Point to specific parts of the output that help you arrive at your conclusion.

   (c) Time-series analysts refer to a bivariate model like this as a "static" regression. Can you guess why? In other words, does this model capture the lingering effects that consumer confidence might have in future months of approval? Is this a big problem or a small problem?

4. Using the data set Ch12TS.sav, estimate a Koyck model of the effects of "ICS" on "Appr" as in Figure 12.10 – that is, including a lagged dependent variable in the model. Answer the following questions:

   (a) What does the output tell you about the cumulative effects of a one-point shift in consumer confidence on President Clinton's approval ratings? How does this compare to the effects estimated in the previous question?

   (b) Examining the SPSS output, how well does the model fit the data? Point to specific parts of the output that help you arrive at your conclusion. How do these model fit statistics compare to the fit statistics in the previous question?

   (c) What concerns might you still have about the model you just estimated?

5. Using the data set Ch12TS.sav, estimate a regression model of the effects of ΔICS on ΔAppr – that is, a model in first differences. (You will have to create those variables using the procedures described in this chapter.) Answer the following questions:

   (a) What does the output tell you about the effects of month-to-month changes in consumer confidence on month-to-month changes in President Clinton's approval ratings? How does this compare to the effects estimated in the previous two questions?

   (b) Examining the SPSS output, how well does the model fit the data? Point to specific parts of the output that help you arrive at your conclusion. How do these model fit statistics compare to the fit statistics in the previous two questions? Does this make these models better or worse than the ones in previous questions?

    (c)   If you were to include a lagged dependent variable in this model, what would that coefficient represent? (Choose your words very precisely!)

6.   Using the data set Ch12TS.sav, estimate two separate Koyck models of the effects of "Pocket" and "BusFut" on "Appr." Answer the following questions:

    (a)   What does the output tell you about the effects of each of these components of consumer confidence on President Clinton's approval ratings? How do these results compare to the results for the overall ICS?

    (b)   Now estimate a model that includes *both* "Pocket" and "BusFut." How do these results compare to those just above? What might explain those differences?

    (c)   How highly correlated are "Pocket" and "BusFut?" Why might this be relevant?

BIBLIOGRAPHY

Bansak, Kirk, Jens Hainmueller and Dominik Hangartner. 2016. "How economic, humanitarian, and religious concerns shape European attitudes toward asylum seekers." *Science* 354(6309): aag2147.

De Mesquita, Bruce Bueno, James D. Morrow, Randolph M. Siverson and Alastair Smith. 1999. "An institutional explanation of the democratic peace." *American Political Science Review* 93(4): 791–807.

Fair, Ray C. 1978. "The effect of economic events on votes for president." *Review of Economics and Statistics* 60: 159–173.

Fortunato, David, Randolph T. Stevenson and Greg Vonnahme. 2016. "Context and political knowledge: Explaining cross-national variation in partisan left–right knowledge." *Journal of Politics* 78(4): 1211–1228.

Heberlig, Eric, Marc Hetherington and Bruce Larson. 2006. "The price of leadership: Campaign money and the polarization of congressional parties." *Journal of Politics* 68(4): 992–1005.

King, Gary, Benjamin Schneer and Ariel White. 2017. "How the news media activate public expression and influence national agendas." *Science* 358(6364): 776–780.

Lipsmeyer, Christine S. and Heather Nicole Pierce. 2011. "The eyes that bind: Junior ministers as oversight mechanisms in coalition governments." *Journal of Politics* 73(4): 1152–1164.

O'Brien, Diana Z. 2015. "Rising to the top: Gender, political performance, and party leadership in parliamentary democracies." *American Journal of Political Science* 59(4): 1022–1039.

Stasavage, David. 2005. "Democracy and education spending in Africa." *American Journal of Political Science* 49(2): 343–358.

Titiunik, Rocio. 2016. "Drawing your senator from a jar: Term length and legislative behavior." *Political Science Research and Methods* 4(2): 293–316.

INDEX

Printed in the United States
by Baker & Taylor Publisher Services